FLYING TO
THE EDGE

FLYING TO THE EDGE

The Groundbreaking Career of Test Pilot
Duncan Menzies

MATTHEW WILLIS

AMBERLEY

First published 2017

Amberley Publishing
The Hill, Stroud
Gloucestershire, GL5 4EP

www.amberley-books.com

British Library Cataloguing in Publication Data.
A catalogue record for this book is available from the British Library.

ISBN 978 1 4456 6441 5 (print)
ISBN 978 1 4456 6442 2 (ebook)

Typeset in 10pt on 13pt Sabon.
Origination by Amberley Publishing.
Printed in the UK.

Contents

Introduction and Acknowledgements

Duncan Menzies would become, over the course of a three-decade career, one of the most respected test pilots in the British aviation industry, making his mark during a period of dramatic change. When the youthful Menzies first took the controls of an aircraft, it was in a wooden-framed biplane built during the First World War. When he retired from working in aviation, the jet age was well underway.

In that time his skill, and a measure of luck, brought him safely through an engine failure in a snowstorm, an aircraft breaking up around him in a high-speed dive and the constant dangers of testing new aircraft on a daily basis. From the 1920s to the 1950s, this methodical, unassuming man was at the forefront of British aviation and did an immense amount to ready the RAF and Fleet Air Arm for war. The records he set and numerous 'firsts' he established came almost incidentally. The great contribution Menzies made to advancing British aviation in the 1930s and '40s, however, did not. Many young pilots in that period will have had reason to thank Duncan Menzies, if they only knew it. Yet his name is far less well known than some of his contemporaries, the 'rock star' test pilots of the 1940s, '50s and '60s, with their records and derring-do carried out in the white heat not just of technology but the public gaze. Telling his story, as fully as the available records allow, for the first time has been a rare privilege.

There are many people to thank for that privilege. First and foremost are Duncan's surviving children, Mary Ann Bennett and Peter Menzies. It was Mary Ann who first contacted me in response to a request for information about the Fairey Fulmar in the Fleet Air Arm Officers Association newsletter, and has been very kind and helpful in unearthing letters, memories and memorabilia. Peter, too, has been amazingly helpful, providing much of the material that has enabled me to build up a picture of Duncan's career, sharing memories, contacting family members and others with a connection and helping me collect their stories. Peter's efforts are the foundation on which this biography of his father has been constructed. Thanks to both Mary Ann and Peter for allowing access to, and publication of, Duncan's documents and photographs.

David Weston, who owns the de Havilland DH87B Hornet Moth that Duncan undertook the first landing at Ringway Airport in, scanned Duncan's complete log books and made the scans available to me, and I am indebted to him for this.

Duncan Simpson, Duncan Menzies' nephew, the Hawker test pilot who was inspired to follow in his uncle's footsteps, kindly shared his experiences and thoughts on the career of his relation.

Captain Eric 'Winkle' Brown, who sadly died in 2016, very helpfully shared his recollections of working with Duncan on trials of naval aircraft, when the former was a test pilot and Menzies was transitioning from test pilot into Fairey's liaison with the Fleet Air Arm, as well as giving some invaluable insights into the problems experienced with the Barracuda and Firefly. Dave Gledhill, former RAF Phantom pilot, provided very useful information about instrument flying. I have reproduced some comments from an interview I made with Lieutenant Commander Chris Götke AFC of the Royal Navy Historic Flight about the Fairey Swordfish, and I thank him for those.

I would also like to thank Robert Paterson, Peter and Mary Ann's cousin, who helpfully recounted some anecdotes Duncan had shared with him, which threw valuable light on several episodes from his RAF career.

I am also indebted to George Jenks, historian with the Avro Heritage Museum, for the information about individual aircraft histories, and to Michael Hancock, Manchester Airport Archivist, for access to the airport's historical files.

Many others have helped including Bob Sikkel who provided information about the No. 92 Squadron escort to Churchill's flight, as witnessed by Duncan in the dark days of 1940. Chris Howard shared memories of conversations with Duncan that shed light on the man and episodes of his career. Like No. 47 (B) Squadron mapping out the unknown interior of Sudan, I have had to fill in gaps in the record. All these people, including any I may have forgotten to mention, have been my cartographers. I thank you all.

Prologue

On 2 February 1941, Flight Lieutenant Duncan Menzies flew to the edge – and over it.

It was a wintry afternoon when the solitary Fairey Fulmar lifted off the runway at Manchester's Ringway airport into the cold air. The pilot, wearing the white cotton flying helmet that marked him out as having served in the RAF in the Middle East, scanned the scene and adjusted the throttle for best climbing speed. The Fulmar lifted away from the Earth, which was mottled with patches of snow, and its undercarriage folded away into the belly of the airframe.

A few weeks beforehand, Fulmars almost identical to the one now ascending into the hard grey sky had been desperately battling the Luftwaffe and the Regia Aeronautica in the crucible of the Mediterranean. Waves of Axis aircraft pummelled the aircraft carrier HMS *Illustrious*, as well as the other ships of Force A and the convoy they were protecting. The Fulmar crews gave their all. They shot down eight torpedo- and dive-bombers, but it wasn't enough to stop five bombs hitting the carrier, 126 of their shipmates being killed. The Fulmars were the first fighter aircraft operated by the Royal Navy to gain the Merlin engines and eight machine-gun armaments of the RAF's Spitfires and Hurricanes, but on that day they had been too slow to climb to stop the worst of the attacks, and not fast enough to chase down the multiplicity of targets.

The scene over Cheshire that February afternoon could hardly be more different. No enemy aircraft harried the lone Fulmar. It did not struggle up from a pitching carrier deck on a heaving sea, but rose from a wide, grassy aerodrome more accustomed to airliners and touring aeroplanes. The pilot was alone, his only passenger being ballast to simulate the weight of a person in the rear cockpit.

His job was to try and make those Fulmars in the Mediterranean and their replacements that bit better, to help them get into the sky that much faster and to help them stay a fraction more controllable at the extremes. The Fulmar's propeller had been altered with a modification developed by the factory. It had brought a slight improvement but caused knock-on effects elsewhere – instability had crept back into the Fulmar's behaviour. The task of the day's flight was to examine those effects and try to establish a solution.

The pilot was not a member of a front line air arm, but he was still fighting the war. His job was to give the combat pilots the best tools with which to fight the enemy. Duncan Menzies was a test pilot.

Around 15 minutes after the wheels had left the runway, the pilot levelled off, having reached perhaps 15,000 ft. He scribbled a note on the pad strapped to his thigh, clipped the pencil into its retainer and tipped the Fulmar into a steep dive.

Almost immediately, the rudder began vibrating. It started to shake rapidly from side to side with the innocuous-sounding phenomenon 'flutter'. The pilot jammed his feet on the rudder bar with all his strength. He could not stop the rudder shaking. Then, as the aircraft continued to plummet earthwards, the elevators began to vibrate in sympathy with the rudder, wrenching the 'stick' backwards and forwards violently. All the pilot's strength could not overcome the flutter. The controls had become rock hard and ceased to work. The aircraft no longer answered its pilot's commands.

The Fulmar hurtled downwards, going 150 mph faster than it could ever manage in level flight. The vicious vibration from the tail surfaces reached the aircraft's limit. Carefully calculated aerodynamics fell off the edge of the page. The aircraft's nose snapped downward.

The only thing that could happen now was total structural failure.

Drawn, heat-treated longerons and stringers snapped like matchwood. Alclad plating tore like paper. The entire tail of the Fulmar broke away from the force of the air. It ripped the aircraft to pieces.

The limits of the pilot's Sutton harness had also been reached, and exceeded – twenty times the force of gravity. As the aircraft folded up and blew apart in the skies over Cheshire, Duncan Menzies broke through the webbing straps, through the acrylic canopy and flew into space.

PART 1

EMPIRE OF DESERT

Flying is not the point. The aeroplane is a means, not an end. It is not for the plane that we risk our lives. Nor is it for the sake of his plough that the farmer ploughs. But through the plane we can leave the cities and their accountants, and find a truth that farmers know.

Antoine de Saint-Exupéry

Chapter 1

Farmer to Flier, 1905–27

On 17 December 1905, a boy was born into a prominent Scottish farming family, the Menzies' of Sutherland, in the north of the country. The Menzies clan is widely believed to have originated after the Norman Conquest, when the family's progenitors sallied forth from Mesnières-en-Bray near the ancient city of Rouen to join the Conqueror. By the twelfth century their descendants had made their home in Scotland, but the early history of the clan is lost in time. Castle Menzies, sacked and burned in the Middle Ages, forfeited much of the clan archive to fire and conflict.

The clan's ancestral home is in Perthshire, the huge central county that spans the lower highlands and expanses of farmland in the east. Pastoral farming naturally became a significant part of the clan's activities. It was the latter country that would be most familiar to a spur of the clan who had made their way well to the north of the clan's traditional seat. These Menzies farmers made their home within the area of the county of Sutherland, a huge area of the Scottish Highlands abutting the Moray Firth and the point where the North Sea meets the Atlantic Ocean. By the turn of the twentieth century, James Menzies was the head of that family.

In the late nineteenth century, James had been sent to New Zealand by his father to learn techniques of sheep farming developed in the colony. There, James met Jess Middleton, a first generation immigrant to the country, and later the couple were married. In time, James took over the farm from his father.

In 1905, Jess bore James a son, whom they named Duncan, to add to the two daughters born previously. In Duncan, James now had an heir to join him in the management of the family's extensive lands around the family home near Rogart and perhaps, eventually, to take them over as he had from his own father. James had enlarged the farm by leasing large tracts of additional land from the Duke of Sutherland, which were also devoted to the family's flocks. Sheep farming was in the family's blood and woven into the fabric of the land Duncan was born into for many generations. The name 'Rogart' itself is derived from the Celtic for 'great enclosed field'.

The family, regarded as a notable part of Scottish society in the early twentieth century, can have had little idea that the newest member would one day exchange his ancient birthright for a thoroughly modern calling on a career path that barely existed at the time he was born. His living was made not on the land but in the skies.

Indeed, the future career-flier, in his childhood and youth, fully expected to become a sheep farmer like his father. Duncan's father James owned a great deal of land, and rented yet more from the Duke of Sutherland. Everything in Duncan's life had led toward him following his father's footsteps.

Duncan was educated at home by a governesses until 1913, when he was sent as a boarder to the Alton Burn prep school near Nairn (now part of the Alton Burn Hotel), where he stayed for six years. Duncan's spell at Alton Burn encompassed the years of the First World War. A former pupil, David Cecil Hope Macbrayne, a 2nd-Lt with No. 11 Squadron, Royal Flying Corps, was killed in action on 21 June 1917. Was Duncan aware of Macbrayne, the 'tumult in the clouds' above the Western Front? There is no evidence yet of any interest in aviation. What little we know of Duncan's childhood suggests an interest in golf and cricket, and a talent for the bagpipes.

In 1919 Duncan left Alton Burn for Loretto School, an institution founded in 1827 in Musselburgh, East Lothian, one of the most prestigious schools in Scotland. It is here that the available evidence begins to indicate how capable the young Duncan Menzies could be. At Loretto he became a prefect, a member of the First XI cricket and a pipe major. He left the school in 1924 at the age of eighteen, and again, his path appeared to indicate nothing but a future in sheep farming.

Duncan Menzies, *c.* 1925.
(Menzies family collection)

He returned to the family lands, learning the trade and spending a period as a so-called 'mud student'. This term typically refers to a trainee farmer but in Scotland it has a particular sense of learning the trade from the ground up, acting as a farmhand. Again, little of Duncan's experiences in this period of his life are known, but during his long career in aviation he was noted for being comfortable with people from all social classes, in what was still a very stratified society even at the time of his retirement. It is possible that Duncan's spell as a 'mud student' helped him be at ease with those he met, whatever their background. Or perhaps that was just in his nature.

The year after he left school, Duncan was given complete responsibility for running a section of the Menzies estates. This he maintained for two years. It was to be an important part of his training and preparation to eventually take over the farm in its entirety. It seems Duncan was keen to take on the responsibility, and it might have settled his course as a sheep farmer.

Instead, the experience seems to have had the opposite effect. During the two years of running his assigned part of the estate, Duncan clashed with his father. The dispute was over methods of farming. Duncan realised he would not have the freedom to pursue the profession as he wished, and began to reconsider his future. It seems that Duncan was not happy to pursue a course if it meant not following his instincts on the best way to carry it out.

Here, as before, the origin of Duncan's desire to fly is a mystery. There is the tiniest hint that a neighbour – indeed, James' landlord, the 5th Duke of Sutherland – may provide an answer.

George Sutherland-Leveson-Gower had been the Under Secretary to Sir Samuel Hoare, the First Secretary of State for Air under the government of Sir Stanley Baldwin, from 1922 to 1924. The Duke contributed greatly to the popularity of the still-new Royal Air Force as a career. It was said that his 'hospitality, enthusiasm, and social position made the Air Force a huge social – and therefore popular – success'.[i]

What Duncan's younger son Peter describes as 'a family legend' suggests that he spoke to the Duke about what he might do next. Dunrobin Castle, the Duke's seat, was around 20 miles from the Menzies home at Rogart, so a meeting could have taken place. On the other hand, James Menzies' was the Duke's tenant, and so it is unclear how much support Duncan could have expected from that quarter. Ultimately, there is nothing but the 'family legend' to indicate that the Duke had any hand in steering Duncan towards the RAF directly. The Duke's enthusiastic public advocacy for the RAF in his role with the Air Ministry might have been enough by itself to influence Duncan's decision.

Whatever the reason, at some point in 1927, the twenty-one-year-old Duncan took the bold step of leaving his chosen career and finding a new one, at least for the time being. The path chosen was to join the Royal Air Force. From that point, his course was set.

Chapter 2

Tyro Pilot, 1927–28

Like all would-be Royal Air Force pilots, Duncan had to pass an entrance exam and a medical. For these, he would probably have travelled to London, to the RAF's then headquarters at Adastral House, on Kingsway in Holborn, or possibly the RAF College at Cranwell. There was the test of knowledge and ability – maths, trigonometry, and a discussion with a panel of senior officers to determine what sort of chap you were. According to an account by Duncan's nephew, Robert Paterson, Menzies' career was almost over before it began:

> Uncle Duncan told me that as a young man he had determined to join the RAF. He left the family home in Rogart, Sutherland and travelled down to sit an entrance 'exam' for the RAF. He did not relate what the component parts of the 'exam' were but they presented no problem to him. The 'exam' culminated in a visit to the C.O.'s office where Duncan duly presented himself. The C.O. was seated behind his desk which Duncan came and stood in front of while the C.O. studied him. There was a brief exchange of words as to how Uncle Duncan had fared in the 'exam'. The C.O. then slid a book across the desk so that the leading edge of the book protruded slightly beyond the lip of the desk on Duncan's side. He balanced a pencil on top of the book, the pencil standing vertically. He invited Uncle Duncan to lift the book from the desk, up to head height and down again, without the pencil falling over. I am not sure if it is widely known but Duncan was born with a shaky hand. It was a condition he was to have all his life. The inevitable happened instantly, for as soon as Duncan grasped the book his shaky hand caused the pencil to fall over. He had failed!
>
> To say that he was unhappy does not convey the extreme feeling he had. He was furious. He returned home but was determined to conquer this task. He found a book and pencil and practised for several hours on a daily basis, trying to lift the book with a pencil balanced on it, to head height and back again. He eventually managed, even with his shaky hand, to execute this manoeuvre flawlessly. He re-applied and returned for his second attempt. The format was exactly the same; same C.O., same book and pencil. This time Uncle Duncan sailed through that part of the 'exam' with ease. He had passed!
>
> He had some particularly biting and pithy comments about, in his opinion, the futile and useless interview techniques that were employed.[ii]

Mary Ann Bennett, Duncan's daughter, recalled that the officer who had nearly cost Menzies his chance was Lt-Col. Norman MacEwen, later Air Chief Marshal Sir Norman MacEwen. This was none other than the Air Ministry's Deputy Director of Training, and Duncan later became friends with MacEwen's son, Ken, who was also a pilot in the RAF.[1]

In press reports of RAF appointments in December 1927, 'D. Menzies' was named among a list of pilot officers posted to the RAF Depot at Uxbridge on appointment to a Short Service Commission, effective 9 December.

The RAF that Menzies had just been admitted to was in a state of stability between two periods of upheaval – the mass demobilisation at the end of the First World War, and the period of modernisation and expansion in the 1930s. In 1923, the service had been compelled to fight for its life, the efforts led by Chief of the Air Staff, Sir Hugh Trenchard. The RAF underwent a dramatic scaling-back in the immediate aftermath of the First World War, with the demobilisation of 23,000 officers, 21,000 cadets and 227,000 other ranks by March 1920, leaving a mere 3,280 officers and 25,000 other ranks.[iii] To add to the effects of this severe shrinking, a concerted effort was made by the Admiralty in the early 1920s to recover control of naval aviation, which it had lost when the Royal Naval Air Service (RNAS) was merged with the army's Royal Flying Corps (RFC) and both arms separated from their parent services to form the RAF in 1918. If the Fleet Air Arm, as the naval branch of military aviation became known, had been removed in 1922–23, it would have threatened the sustainability of the independent air force, especially if Army Co-Operation Squadrons had also been placed under direct Army control again, as some in that service wanted.[iv] As it was, the independence of the RAF and the role of the Air Ministry in naval aviation and Army Co-operation was confirmed in 1923. Nevertheless, during a time of increasing austerity, it was vital for the RAF to be able to demonstrate its value in order to protect it from cuts or total disbandment.

There were two aspects of the RAF that helped ensure its survival in the early 1920s, and which had a direct impact on Duncan Menzies' career with the service. Those were the development of the RAF into a force for colonial policing, and the introduction of the Short Service Commission.

When the existence of the RAF was confirmed, peacetime austerity forced certain conditions onto it. The regular service would remain small, highly trained and specialised. To supplement it, short commissions were introduced whereby applicants would give five years of full-time service upon completion of training, after which they would join the reserve. This enabled an adequate level of recruitment and the creation of an additional body of trained men that could supplement the small core of regular personnel in the event of war or escalating international tensions. Importantly, the policy would also enhance the RAF's ability to expand in the future, should the need and opportunity arise.

All regular RAF officers would train at Cranwell for two years, while those on Short Service Commissions would be posted to a Flying Training School (FTS) in the UK or overseas, where they would train for a year.[2] The five-year Short Service Commission was later criticised as it meant trained officers leaving the Air Force when they were still able to give more years of service. However, at the time, the system enabled the RAF to recruit sufficient numbers of officers to maintain its commitments and prove the value of an independent air force. The creation of Medium Service Commissions a few years later helped to address the problem of retaining trained officers – and some short service personnel were permitted to extend their commission from five to ten years if they were of the required standard. The officer ranks of the RAF, unlike the Royal Navy or the Army, were chiefly made up of short service personnel in the mid-1920s. It was vital to the service that it remained an attractive career choice to young men of ability and drive. The RAF emphasised the skills and personal qualities that Short Service Commissions would confer on the holder, making them attractive to employers in the engineering industry or related fields. Pay was relatively generous, at 15s 2d a day while on probation, and after eighteen months most pilot officers could expect promotion to flying officer, whereupon pay rose to 18s 10d per day, rising to 21s 18d per day after two years in the service. Furthermore, a gratuity of £375 was paid at the end of the commission. The enthusiasm of those such as the Duke of Sutherland also gave the RAF vital social cachet, which at the time has been likened by some commentators to that of a prestigious Guards regiment in the Army (*see note*[i]).

In 1919, Trenchard set out his vision for the RAF over the coming period in a document entitled 'Permanent Organization of the RAF – Note by the Secretary of State for Air on a Scheme Outlined by the Chief of Staff'. In this, the 'first duty of the RAF', as paraphrased by Winston Churchill, Minister for Air, was 'to garrison the Empire'. This was crucial to the future and the shape of the peacetime RAF in the light of the 'Ten Year Rule', the principle which stated that Britain would not fight a major war for a decade. This shifted the focus from home defence or expeditionary war to 'colonial policing' – maintaining the reach of London across the vast open spaces of the Empire, dealing with rebellions and unrest, and deterring invaders. Thus it was that, in 1927, the RAF's focus was substantially on the Middle East, Africa, India and the North-West frontier, and it was not surprising that Pilot Officer Duncan Menzies was one of around eighty officers a year posted to No. 4 Flying Training School (4 FTS) based in Egypt to train as an RAF pilot.

In January 1928, Menzies sailed on the Ellerman Hall Line steamer SS *City of Cairo* from Liverpool to Port Said with twenty-seven other recruits. From there he travelled to Abu Sueir, 14 miles west of Ismailia, to join 4 FTS.

No. 4 Flying Training School was established in April 1921. It was effectively a training centre for the RAF in North and North-West Africa and the Middle East, sending crews trained in every discipline out to squadrons operating all over that vast area. The FTS was broken into a number of Flights, each responsible for different aspects of training, which included, over the length of the course, the theory of flight, rigging, engines, elementary wireless theory and operation, meteorology and navigation. The Flights were broken into *ab initio* training – learning to fly – and service training, where students began to specialise into a role such as fighter or bomber pilot. When the FTS was founded, it was equipped with Bristol F2B Fighter aircraft and undertook training in army co-operation. In April 1922, a flight of Avro 504Ks was added for *ab initio* training, and this was dubbed 'B' Flight, while the original part of the unit formed 'A' Flight. Around the same time, 'C' Flight was established with Airco DH.9A aircraft for day bombing training. 'A' Flight later gained Vickers Vimy heavy bombers, which then split off to form the basis of 'F' Flight.

The RAF Depot at Aboukir was equipped to rebuild aircraft, and many 4 FTS aircraft were rebuilt there either to a modern standard or to enable them to carry out training more effectively, such as fitting them with dual controls.

Although 4 FTS' central base was the aerodrome at Abu Sueir, it also used a number of basic landing grounds in the vicinity. Landing grounds such as these (which did not even warrant the name of airfield or aerodrome) were essential to RAF operations in the Middle East and North Africa. The distances between centres were so great that many small landing grounds, with roughly prepared airstrips and minimal facilities, were placed all over the territory to provide landing places in the event of emergency, or as staging posts in longer flights.

Menzies made his first flight as an RAF officer as a passenger in a DH.9A, E9688, on 23 January. The pilot was Flying Officer Riccard and the flight was a cross-country to Suez via Ismailia. The next day, with the same pilot, he flew from Abu Sueir to Cairo and Helwan, returning on the 25th. Menzies' first few days were spent familiarising himself from the air with the territory around Abu Sueir in a DH.9A.

Most of his basic training was conducted, however, on the venerable Avro 504K, referred to as the 'Avro "Mono"' in Menzies' log books on the basis that it was powered by the 80 hp Gnome Monosoupape (single valve) rotary engine. From this point on it was a case of learning by doing. Of the next fifteen flights Duncan made, all but one saw him take the controls at some point.

A fellow Short Service Commission officer training at 4 FTS with Menzies was Richard Sydney Ubee. He had sailed to Canada to work on the railways, hefting sleepers and rails in sub-zero temperatures, then had gone back to London to work in a Rootes dealership, before taking exception to a senior employee demanding more deference than Ubee was prepared to offer and joining the RAF instead. Ubee appears in a photograph with Duncan during a period of leave in Troodos, smiling in their uniforms and holding up a fox skin, its legs ludicrously still attached and sticking out on each side. Ubee also later became a test pilot, eventually reaching the rank of Air Vice-Marshal. He was interviewed by the Imperial War Museum in 1992, and the recording gives an insight into the training at 4 FTS:

> I was posted to 4 FTS in Egypt, which was a flying training school. I went there; we learned to fly on Avro 504K. That was the training machine of the time. The 504K was a little two-seater with a rotary engine. It was just the aeroplane for the job ... You got fined if you buggered around. If you blipped the engine, coming in, to keep it running, the instructor would make a note and you were fined, I think it was five or ten *piastres*. But they were good training aeroplanes. In the second term we modernised, went up from the 'K' to the 'L'[3] and that had a static engine, a Lynx I think, or something of that order ... And they were much more favourable because they ticked over, you see, not a rotary engine but a radial engine.[v]

The Monosoupape could not be throttled as most engines were, and the only way to adjust the power in the glide was to use the 'blip' switch, which temporarily cut the ignition, but as the fuel supply did not also cut out, it was possible to damage the engine through overuse – no doubt the reason for the fines imposed on trainee pilots using it! Any damage to the aeroplane would certainly have seen the pilot fined: half a crown for a heavy landing that bent an axle, 7s 6d for a broken tailskid, and God forbid a written-off aircraft or one that had to go back to the depot – the students would have reacted to any fellow committing such a sin with great hilarity, and entries in the 'fine book' would be the source of much amusement.

Duncan Menzies and Richard Sydney Ubee, a fellow student pilot, on leave in Cyprus in 1928. Ubee later became a test pilot at the Royal Aircraft Establishment and an Air Vice-Marshal. (Menzies family collection)

Menzies first flight in the venerable Avro 504 was a 30-minute flight in aircraft F8709 on 30 January with instructor Flight Lieutenant Greenslade, which covered basic use of the controls, straight flying and gentle turns. Approaching the Avro for the first dual control flight, we can imagine the scenario: the waft of Castrol R, the blast of air as the throttle is opened up, the ground falling away below, nerves triggering nausea as he struggles to hear the pilot through the rudimentary intercom. How is the aircraft handling? Does it answer the controls as he thinks it will, or is he overcompensating, progressive in a series of jolts and bounces? Did he wear the wrong shoes, giving no feel for the rudder bar, an error which students occasionally fell foul of. Does the sideslip before landing catch him out, the ground suddenly approaching from the wrong angle, a surprising gale of slipstream over the rim of the cockpit?

The following day, Menzies and Greenslade undertook a 25-minute flight in the Humber-built 504K E4205, learning about 'gliding angle and best climbing angle', according to Menzies' log book. Duncan was getting the hang of it fast.

In the first week of February, Menzies' training covered the basics – take-offs, landings, turns, taxiing. On 7 February Menzies got his first taste of a spin, with practice spins in the right-hand direction. (This was the easier direction to recover from, given the clockwise rotation of the engine). The stall is followed by the sickening sense of the aircraft dropping, no longer supported by the air, the wing sagging, the aircraft whipping round, the G-forces pressing against the side of the cockpit. A totally different feeling to any Menzies had yet experienced; a thousand feet lost in moments.

After a by-now rare flight where Duncan was merely a passenger on the 8 February, and 10 minutes of circling the aerodrome, it was back to dual-control flying with the more difficult left-hand spins.

Duncan was making one or two flights a day by now, usually of around a half-hour's duration first thing in the morning. He would have also been engaged in a great deal of other study concerning engineering, navigation, theory of flight and other matters. In fact, at this point flying made up a relatively small part of his day, even though he made at least one flight on every weekday bar one for the first three weeks.

There was clearly more to life than training at Abu Sueir. The trainee aircrews tended to live in hut accommodation rather than the tents common at some aerodromes, and facilities were relatively good, including a swimming pool. Activities while off duty included playing cricket or tennis, or simply relaxing at the 'Club' and its beer garden.

After just under 12 hours in the air, and less than a month after his flying training began, Menzies went solo in an Avro 504K. The flight took place on 9 February 1928, and involved take-off, a 10-minute flight, and landing. It was his eighteenth flight.

If Menzies was nervous about his first solo, there is no evidence of it. A photograph survives that marks the occasion, showing Menzies in the cockpit, wearing a fur-lined flying helmet. He is looking confident, if unsmiling. Two more photographs relate to Duncan's second solo – the first shows him posing with his instructor, Flight Lieutenant Greenslade, standing in front of the aircraft he first soloed in. This time Duncan is grinning. A third image shows Menzies in the cockpit once more, with Greenslade walking around the port wing, and marked, 'Just off for second solo.' This was the following day, 10 February, and was a 25-minute flight in which Duncan ascended to 2,000 ft and practised turns.

That Avro 504K was the first 504 Menzies had flown in. The photographs show that it was marked 'E8709' but was in fact F8709. It had evidently had an incorrect serial applied by the FTS 'erks' when it was delivered. This Avro was actually something of an antique by the time of Duncan's solo. It had been built under licence by George Parnall & Co. Ltd at that company's factory at Yate, near Bristol, in the last year of the First World War as part of the large orders of aircraft that were soon to become surplus to requirements. According to Avro Heritage historian George Jenks, 'It probably went directly into store until sent to the Packing Depot at Ascot. After shipping to Egypt it was assembled at the Air Depot at Aboukir and delivered to No. 4 FTS at Abu Sueir.'[vi]

In fact, most of the Avro 504K aircraft Menzies flew during his initial training were aircraft that had been ordered and built during the First World War but stored for most of their lives, due to the Armistice rendering them surplus. When the RAF had need of them in peacetime, they would be taken out of storage and transported to a Packing Depot to be dismantled and crated. They would then be shipped to the depot at Aboukir for assembly, and delivered to their unit.

Pilot Officer Duncan Menzies about to make his first solo flight on 9 February 1928. (Menzies family collection)

Menzies and his instructor, Flight Lieutenant Greenslade, in front of (wrongly marked) Avro 504K F8709 before Menzies' second solo flight on 10 February 1928. (Menzies family collection)

The Avro 504 series enjoyed astonishing longevity. It first went into production in 1913 and continued, with relatively small changes, until the last aircraft was delivered in 1932. The 504K was gradually supplanted by the 504N, which was powered by an Armstrong Siddeley Lynx seven-cylinder radial (stationary) engine and fitted with oleo-leg undercarriage, but which was otherwise similar to the First World War-vintage version. The Avro 504s were not phased out of service with 'B' Flight 4 FTS until April 1936, when they were replaced with the more modern Avro Tutor.

After Menzies had gotten to grips with solo flying, the training became more intensive and more closely related to real conditions. On 13 February, 50 minutes of flying, dual and solo, was devoted to landing on a circle marked out on the aerodrome. Then the focus was on turning with reference to a fixed point on the ground, all intended to improve Menzies' control and precision. (These flights were made in Avro 504K H3093, built by Brush Coaches, a company normally known for building railway rolling stock.) The next few weeks were a mix of dual and solo control, and the by-now usual mix of take-offs and landings, spins and turns interspersed with more specific training. The flying started, tentatively, to move beyond Abu Sueir as well, with occasional flights to landing grounds in the surrounding country.

Towards the end of the month, Menzies got his first taste of aerobatics – a discipline at which he would soon excel. On 29 February, his log book is marked 'half rolls'. In the RAF terminology of the time, the half-roll was equivalent to what is now known as the 'Split-S', where the pilot rolls the aircraft inverted and pulls through a half-loop, to end up horizontal and flying in the opposite direction. This coincided with more flights to outlying landing grounds, generally operated by 'F' Flight with its Vickers Vimy bombers.

This pattern continued into March, with much of Menzies' flying now taking place at landing grounds outside Abu Sueir. All went smoothly until the 5th, when on a flight back to Abu Sueir from an outlying landing ground the engine of H3093 began to miss, and he was forced to turn back. Then, on 16 March, while Menzies was flying solo to a landing ground, the engine of E4205 failed completely 10 minutes out from Abu Sueir. Fortunately, forced-landing practice took up a significant amount of Menzies' flying training.

Menzies cannot have been under any illusions as to how dangerous training to fly was. Two photographs in his collection from 1928 shows a wrecked Avro 504N, J8680, which sits on its mangled nose, tail in the air, and fuselage angled drunkenly to the right. On the reverse he has written, 'A pupil's effort (Black).'[4] Who 'Black' is and if anyone was hurt in the crash is not clear, nor if the aircraft was written off. There was one fatal crash during Duncan's training at 4 FTS – Leading Aircraftman (LAC) Sydney Charles Stevens was killed in an incident involving an Avro. It is notable that in the photographs of Menzies' early flights at Abu Sueir none of the aircrew appear to be wearing parachutes, indicating that they were not in widespread use in 1928. (The first 'live' 4 FTS parachute jump did not take place until 1930.)

The apparent risks, however, do not appear to have dulled Menzies' enthusiasm for aerobatic flying – in March he added looping to the half-rolls being practised. Nevertheless, the dangers were manifold. Two weeks after his engine failure, Menzies' training was temporarily suspended while he took part in a search for a missing pilot,

Labelled 'a pupil's effort' in Menzies's photo album, this shows the remains of Avro 504N J8680 after a crash at Abu Sueir. (Menzies family collection)

making two half-hour flights in Avro H3093, once again showing how potentially risky flying over desert could be, even relatively close to the large aerodrome at Abu Sueir.

In May, Menzies completed his *ab initio* training with a test on the 3rd of the month. This consisted of a 45-minute flight with instructor Flight Lieutenant Greenslade. This he passed, meaning he could progress to advanced training after 41 hours 45 minutes solo and 59 hours 30 minutes flying total to date. His log book bears the caption 'Transferred to "C" Flight DH.9s', signed by the 4 FTS Chief Instructor and dated 3 May (although Duncan carried out two more flights with Avros of 'B' Flight on the 3rd and 4th, covering slightly more advanced techniques including stalling turns and use of instruments, interestingly with Flight Lieutenant Bates, an instructor with 'C' Flight).

'C' Flight, which Menzies had been transferred to, provided advanced training for day bomber pilots. The Flight operated Airco (Aircraft Manufacturing Company) DH.9As, which were much larger and heavier machines than the Avro, and were affectionately referred to in Menzies' log book as 'Ninaks'. The DH.9A was a development of the DH.9 bomber of the First World War, itself a development of the successful DH.4. The 9A was an improved DH.9 with increased span wings, strengthened fuselage and, most importantly, an American 400 hp Liberty L-12 twelve-cylinder V engine (replacing the DH.9's unreliable Siddeley Puma). 'C' Flight's machines had, of course, been converted to dual control. Most of the DH.9As Menzies flew at 4 FTS had been built at the end of the First World War, or just after, as most contracts were completed, given that the aircraft had been chosen to equip the post-war RAF. Most of the 'Ninaks' had been brought out of storage, shipped to Egypt and there had been modified to suit local conditions, with long-range fuel tanks, additional coolant radiators, etc., and, when passed from frontline squadrons to 4 FTS, had been adapted to training configuration.

One instructor of the time was quoted as describing DH.9As as 'jolly nice aeroplanes, the only snag being they nearly always catch fire if you prang them'.[vii] They were apparently easy to land, and for a 'comparatively large aeroplane was surprisingly light on the controls', and 'an extremely pleasant if somewhat draughty aeroplane'.[viii]

Menzies' first flight with 'C' Flight was a 10-minute hop as a passenger, in aircraft E8642, with Flight Lieutenant Bates the pilot. Then it was straight on to the business of learning the trade of a day bomber pilot, with a 35-minute dual flight in the same DH.9A. The first two weeks with 'C' Flight was almost entirely devoted to landings and approaches, with the occasional cross-country flight or practice turns thrown in. He soloed on the type on 17 May, with a 10-minute flight in J8097 that involved take-off, a few turns and landing.

A few days after that, following four months at Abu Sueir, Duncan had a month's leave, which he spent in Cyprus. Photographs from that trip to the mountains at Troodos show Duncan and his fellow students relaxing in jackets and ties, camping in the woods at a site apparently run by one 'Ma Snelling', enjoying a 'gin party', and posing with the donkey Ma Snelling used to carry baskets of laundry.

On his return from Cyprus towards the end of June, Menzies continued training on the DH.9A, the routine initially much as it had been in the Avro 504K at 'B' Flight. New elements introduced over time included flying by compass (10 July) and cloud flying (16 July).

On 23 July 1928, Menzies experienced his first crash. This occurred during a solo flight in DH.9A J6967 at Abu Sueir. It was his fourth flight of the day and the third in that aeroplane. No details are available apart from the brief note 'crashed main aerodrome' (underlined in red) in his log book. It does not appear that Menzies was injured, as he was flying again the next day, but that particular aircraft does not feature in his log books again. No information is available on the aircraft's ultimate fate, but it seems likely it was so badly damaged as to need to be returned to the Aboukir depot for repair, or even that it was written off. DH.9A J6967 seems to have been unlucky – two years previously, it was involved in a fatal accident when the pilot, twenty-two-year-old Pilot Officer Ronald William Coneybeer, was struck by the propeller.

Flying went on, despite the accident, and on 1 August 1928 Menzies spun a DH.9A for the first time. Then, a week later, he took and passed his first navigation test. This was followed on 17 August by Menzies' second air pilotage test.[5]

That month, a giant floating dry dock bound for Singapore was towed through the Suez Canal and seems to have caused something of a stir among the 4 FTS crews, as they overflew its slow progress through the canal and Red Sea several times. Duncan took aerial photographs of the dock and its train of tugs (three ahead, two behind) from his DH.9A when it was south of Lake Timsah, and again when it passed through the Great Bitter Lake. Towing the dock through the canal cost £10,000 in fees. It was 855 ft long, 172 ft wide and 75 ft high, covering the area of a football pitch. It had a lifting capacity of 50,000 tons, which would enable the dock to service the largest battleships. It left England in June, and took five months to tow to Singapore. Menzies' photographs indicate how disruptive the floating dock must have been to the normal canal traffic, but it emphasised the global reach of the Empire that the RAF was now helping to maintain.

Menzies' navigation training continued, with the flying broadening into longer flights further afield. On 17 September 1928, he flew a solo triangular cross-country flight from Abu Sueir to the RAF base at Deversoir on the shores of the Great Bitter Lake, El Qantara (written as Kantara in the log book), and back to Abu Sueir, the flight lasting an hour and 10 minutes.

Much of the flying took place at the 'C' Flight landing ground, a little outside Abu Sueir. The basic conditions are apparent from photographs, with crews sitting on the ground, on ammunition cases or in the back of a lorry – there are no facilities evident. The temperature could also drop to uncomfortable levels. One photograph shows 'C' Flight in Sidcot suits, gathered around a fire in an oil can dug into a shallow pit. On the reverse is written 'when the weather was cold and "Sky" was the order.'

From 27 August the use of weaponry entered into Menzies' flying training for the first time. On this date he used a camera gun while flying as a passenger in DH.9A J8142. This was probably a Hythe camera gun, which was available in various marks, and would be fitted in place of an existing machine gun. The Hythe was designed to resemble a Lewis gun in form, operation and weight. The camera was used to record footage of simulated

A rather miserable looking 'landing ground party'. It could be cold in the desert. (Menzies family collection)

air-to-ground or air-to-air gunnery. The following month Menzies began practising flying with bombs – the initial load being two 112 lb bombs. (The DH.9A could carry a maximum of 660 lb, in bombs generally not larger than 230 lb, and the typical load was three 112 lb bombs.) The purpose was simply to accustom the pilot to the handling characteristics of the aircraft when loaded with bombs. The following month the load went up to four 112 lb bombs, which was relatively heavy for the aircraft, although Menzies never actually practised bombing while at 4 FTS. That would have to wait until he joined an operational squadron.

Another milestone was passed on 8 October 1928, when Menzies carried his first passenger. The lucky recipient of a 30-minute ride in DH.9A H156 was LAC Lisle.

On 22 October 1928, after just over 100 hours solo, Menzies successfully passed his training course. His 'Form 895' certificate shows that he scored 83 per cent of the total marks available in flying, and was rated 'above the average' both on the DH.9A and with regard to his general proficiency as a pilot. His Commanding Officer, Wing Commander F. K. Haskins, wrote that Menzies had 'passed a good course and worked hard throughout', adding that he was 'a very good type of junior officer who is categorised as "above the average" on DH.9A aircraft. Very keen'.

Chapter 3

'Above the Average': No. 45 (B) Squadron, Helwan, 1928–29

On 27 October 1928, five days after passing his course (and only two days after the course technically ended), Duncan Menzies joined No. 45 (Bomber) Squadron at Helwan, an RAF airfield south of Cairo.

The collection of Royal Air Force squadrons clustered around the Canal Zone formed a giant hub for distributing air power into Africa and the Middle East. Strings of landing grounds marked out routes South and East.

No. 45 Squadron first formed in the RFC in 1916, equipped with Sopwith 1½ Strutters before re-equipping with Camels in July 1917 and eventually disbanding at the end of 1919. It was reformed in Egypt in 1921 as a transport squadron, later being reduced to a single Flight attached to No. 47 Squadron. No. 45 Squadron was reformed as a full squadron in 1927 as a day bomber squadron that could act as a 'regional reserve' moving to trouble spots to support locally based forces when required. This was part of the highly successful policy of 'Air Control' then being practised by the RAF across the British Empire. Rather appropriately, in view of its service in desert country and its First World War operation of the Sopwith, No. 45 had adopted the camel as its badge. Most of the squadron's DH.9As were marked with a crest bearing this symbol at the time Menzies was a member, despite the fact that it would not be officially recognised until 1936. There was still much linking the squadron to Britain, not least its cricket team. The squadron also had an active athletics squad.

The concept of Air Control was something of a forward-thinking masterstroke on the part of Sir Hugh Trenchard. After the dramatic shrinkage of the immediate post-war period, the RAF did not have the resources or the opportunity to demonstrate its value as a strategic force in a conventional war. The British Empire was, however, spread across a huge area – even more so after the additional territories gained from the Ottoman Empire at the end of the First World War. Maintaining peace and stability within its borders was no easy task, especially at a time of financial difficulties and force reduction. Sayyid Mohammed Abdullah Hassan (disparagingly known in Britain as 'The Mad Mullah') led a resistance, the so-called Dervish State, against British rule in Somaliland from 1899. Four military campaigns had proved completely unable to dislodge Sayyid Mohammed and his supporters, and the year after the end of the First World War the Colonial Office expressed the desire to take action again. Local forces were inadequate, consisting of the Somaliland Camel Corps, the successor to the Somaliland Camel Constabulary, which had been soundly defeated the year before the war. The Army indicated that up to three

The personnel of No. 45 (B) Squadron, RAF Helwan, in 1929, with one of the squadron's DH.9A aircraft. Menzies is on the extreme right of the picture in the middle row. (Menzies family collection)

divisions would be required, with a cost running into millions of pounds. Trenchard seized the opportunity to show what could be done with air power. He offered to fulfil the Colonial Office's requirements with one squadron of Airco DH.9 bombers in addition to the Camel Corps and a small number of additional men and land vehicles.

The mobility of the small force of aircraft, and its ability to strike from the air with relative impunity, not to mention assisting communication between ground forces, achieved what the previous four campaigns could not. The RAF drove Sayyid Mohammed out of the territories he controlled, destroyed his strongholds and ended his influence in Somaliland. As a result, in 1921 the RAF was given responsibility for peacekeeping in Iraq and Transjordan, and placed in charge of all forces stationed there. RAF forces across the Middle East and North and East Africa were also structured in this way, and No. 45 Squadron, with its roving brief, was part of this system of colonial peacekeeping and policing.

Trenchard also encouraged the RAF to pioneer air routes, using air power to connect the Empire in a way that had simply not been possible before, rather than leaving this to civilian operators. The first such route was Cairo–Baghdad, carried out by DH.9As of Nos 47 and 30 Squadrons, and Handley Page 0/400s of No. 70 Squadron, in conjunction with vehicles on the ground. It became the basis of Imperial Airways' network of routes.

Finally, and no less importantly, the RAF was prompted to set point-to-point speed and endurance records between outposts of the Empire wherever operational commitments allowed, thus keeping the service in the headlines and promoting its modernity and effectiveness.

The situation in Egypt was complex at the time Menzies was posted to his first operational unit. Egypt was technically independent, following a period as a British protectorate dating from the First World War, but in reality Britain had a huge influence over, and military presence in, the country. The zone of the Suez Canal was formally under British control. Aside from sporadic nationalist unrest, Egypt was relatively peaceful in the late 1920s, and Britain had signed a treaty with the country's government indicating a long-term aspiration to draw down military forces. Nevertheless, vigilance was required. A 1939 text on colonial policing indicates the atmosphere under which No. 45 Squadron, and the others of the Middle East Command, existed:

> Our long experience of communal troubles in India and elsewhere should have taught us that communal rioting will break out with little warning, and to what length it will go. We know that the firm and impartial intervention of force is the sole means of restoring peace and of preventing the spread of disorder.[ix]

An 'Internal Security Scheme' was in place to cope with anti-British riots by defending sites of importance such as power stations and bridges, and deploying 'flying columns' rapidly from elsewhere.

When Menzies joined No. 45 (B) Squadron he was appointed to 'C' Flight. There was at least one familiar face – his Flight Commander was Flight Lieutenant C. S. Riccard, who had piloted Menzies on his first flight at Abu Sueir. Shortly after Duncan joined the squadron, a new Commanding Officer arrived, Squadron Leader F. J. Vincent DFC. Vincent had been a pilot with the Royal Naval Air Service in the First World War, transferring to the RAF on its inception before serving with Nos 3, 1, 32 and 56 Squadron and being awarded the Distinguished Flying Cross for service during operations in Iraq in 1922. The day after Vincent joined, Menzies flew as his passenger in DH.9A J7093 for a 3½-hour flight to Amman in the Transjordan (modern Jordan), over 300 miles from Helwan. They returned the next day, the West–East flight taking 5 hours 20 minutes. Unfortunately, the reason for this journey is recorded neither in Duncan's log book nor the squadron's Operations Record Book, but it must have been an epic flight, crossing the entire width of Arabia and Palestine.

After this, Menzies' service with the squadron settled into a pattern of local flying around Helwan, training in bombing and gunnery, and night and formation flying. There were also occasional instances of aerial photography, and message dropping and picking-up – the latter an essential part of working with ground forces before the development of effective air-ground radio. It was during this time with No. 45 (B) Squadron, on 1 January 1929, that Duncan received a rare rating of 'average', although Squadron Leader Vincent did not consider that there were any 'special faults' with Menzies' flying that needed to be addressed.

Robert Paterson, Menzies' nephew, recounts a story from this period that shines a light on life as an RAF officer stationed in Egypt at the time, and also on relations between officer and enlisted ranks:

> Uncle Duncan knew I had been in the school pipe band and he himself was a very able piper. We were chatting one evening about piping. He told me that the thing he treasured most about piping occurred when he was stationed in Cairo with the RAF.

J8189 'Old '89', a DH.9A often flown by Menzies, in the air above Helwan. Part of the camp can be seen beyond the aircraft. (Menzies family collection)

Menzies flying 'Old '89' above the desert near Helwan in 1929. Note the squadron crest painted on the engine cowling and, behind it, a spare wheel in case of punctures at far-flung landing grounds. (Menzies family collection)

There had been a dinner in the Officers' Mess. A piper from the local Egyptian pipe band was detailed to play some tunes for the officers' entertainment during that evening. The piper finished his tunes but before he departed one of the officers spoke up and said, 'Menzies, you play the pipes, go on give us a tune.' Uncle Duncan got to his feet and went over to the piper, who gave him his pipes. Uncle Duncan said that you could see it in the piper's eyes – he had to give this officer his pipes. What could this officer possibly know about piping – he was probably praying that his pipes wouldn't get broken.

Uncle Duncan played a few tunes, returned the pipes to the piper and thanked him for the use of them. He said the piper now had a very different expression on his face. Uncle Duncan thought no more about it. The evening came to an end and everyone repaired to their respective tents.

At some ungodly hour in the very early morning Uncle Duncan was woken by someone knocking at his tent (I don't know how you knock at a tent but some means of attracting the occupant's attention was employed). Uncle Duncan went to the tent's entrance and found the piper of the previous evening. He was there with humility and reverence and perhaps a bit of awe. Would Uncle Duncan please, please teach him the tunes that he had played that evening.

Uncle Duncan invited him into the tent and they spent several hours going over the tunes until the piper had them in his head.

Apparently, one of the tunes he played was 'The Muckin' of Geordie's Byre', a comic song from the North of Scotland about a farmer and his family and the accidents that befall them when trying to clean their cowshed.

On 18 January 1929, Duncan was promoted to the rank of Flying Officer.

No. 45 Squadron had, since its reformation, become skilled in endurance flying. (Earlier in the year, No. 45 (B) Squadron had won the Lloyd Cup, an award presented by Lord Lloyd to the Middle East Command squadron awarded the most points for a pre-arranged endurance flight.)

On 12 March 1929, the squadron's Operations Record Book noted:

An endurance flight of 7 hours 10 minutes was carried out by 9 squadron aircraft, the course taken was via – HELWAN – CAIRO – ABOUKIR – CAIRO – PORT-SAID – KANTARA – ISMAILIA – ABU SUEIR – DEVASSOIR – SUEZ – AND HELWAN. Eight aircraft completed the course, one having to land at ABOUKIR owing to engine trouble.[x]

Menzies took part in this flight, with Corporal Spillard his passenger. The squadron carried out this remarkably long flight in formation, demonstrating not only its skill in endurance but also precision. A week later, the officer commanding RAF Middle East Command, Air Vice-Marshal T. I. Webb-Bowen, held his annual inspection of the squadron.

While Duncan spent several days on camera gun training at the end of April 1929, Squadron Leader Vincent and Flight Lieutenant Luke left Helwan to visit a number of sites along the Nile – Aswan, Nag Hammadi, Sohag and Asyut – concerning the Internal Security Scheme. The exact nature of the visits is not clear, but suggests that unrest was still a concern, and that No. 45 Squadron might need to be sent to trouble spots at short notice. Meanwhile, even with Vincent and Luke's absence, the squadron set a record for flying time that month, completing 494 hours and 45 minutes in the air during April – the best since it re-equipped with the DH.9A. The squadron was evidently not unduly concerned about the likelihood of violence, as photographs from 1928–9 show members of the squadron relaxing at the beach at Port Said, 'on rest cure.'

A further re-equipment was imminent, as No. 45 Squadron was soon to give up its DH.9As for the new Fairey IIIF biplane. The IIIF was a much more modern design than the venerable 'Ninak', with a 570 hp Napier Lion engine, mixed wood-metal or all-metal structure (depending on the precise variant), and a more aerodynamically efficient form. On 6 April, Menzies flew Squadron Leader Vincent to Abu Sueir to pick up Fairey IIIF Mk I SR1143 (the 'R' in the serial indicating that it had been rebuilt with an all-metal structure). This aircraft was brought back to the squadron to acclimatise air and ground crews to the type before it was re-equipped. Menzies made numerous flights in SR1143, but on 11 April flew to Abu Sueir to pick up spares for it, indicating there had been a snag or two while the squadron pilots learned its ways. Menzies' time with No. 45 (B) Squadron was drawing to an end, however, and he would be posted elsewhere before the squadron re-equipped. On 8 June, Squadron Leader Vincent noted in Menzies' log book the proficiency rating 'above the average', and three days later Duncan left for No. 47 (B) Squadron at Khartoum, Sudan.

When Menzies left No. 45 (B) Squadron, the unit was preparing to exchange its DH.9As for more modern Fairey IIIFs. This aircraft, SR1143, was used by the squadron to acclimatise the pilots, and is seen here flown by Duncan during its return to Aboukir. (Menzies family collection)

Chapter 4

No. 47 (B) Squadron, Khartoum, 1929–30

In 1928–9, the least stable territory in the Middle East Command was undoubtedly Palestine. Control of that country was on the brink of collapse. However, Sudan was also a region of concern. At the time it was a territory of the Egyptian kingdom, and much of the Egyptian army was stationed there. The RAF presence in Sudan was a bulwark against a repeat of the Mahdist revolt that had convulsed the country in the late nineteenth century – and No. 47 (B) Squadron was more or less the sum total of that presence.

The Nuer people had produced a number of prophets during the British presence there, and had a history of raiding other tribes, particularly of the neighbouring Dinka people. There had also been a nationalist mutiny among the Egyptian army in Sudan in 1925. Sudan was the front line as far as the peacetime RAF was concerned. Amongst Menzies's personal effects saved from his career was a 'quick guide' sheet for a Colt Automatic .455 1911 Government Model pistol. It illustrates the main parts of the gun and gives instructions for its use. If Duncan was issued with a sidearm, it would most likely have been in Sudan (though it could also have been issued for flights traversing 'trouble spots' a year or two later in his career). One can't help but hope that more training in the use of the gun was provided than a simple foolscap instruction sheet.

Sudan was not only the front line but the frontier. Reconnaissance by aircraft of the squadron helped establish air routes and fill in gaps on the maps. There was still literal *terra incognita* in Sudan at the time Menzies was posted there. On one occasion the squadron had found an area of previously uncharted territory where, to everyone's surprise, it was possible to build a road. Efforts to open up the interior and link up with East African colonies were gratefully grasped. As the 1920s gave way to the 1930s, Sudan began to turn from wilderness to something slightly more tamed. No. 47 (B) Squadron blazed the trail, ranging all over the country in its operations from Khartoum, roughly in the centre, skywriting on the blank pages. Menzies family friend Chris Howard recalled that Duncan, 'Showed me some of his log books and one of the maps that he used. They had to make their own maps because before they arrived there weren't any.'[xi]

British colonial policy was largely favourable to the ethnically black peoples of Southern Sudan. The Colonial Office wished to separate those regions from the largely Arab North, with a view to eventually incorporating Southern Sudan into Britain's East African colonies. Two years prior to Menzies' posting to No. 47 (B) Squadron, the Lou Nuers, led by the prophet Guek Ngundeng, rebelled in opposition to the road-building programme, and the British government in Khartoum decided to send a military force

Khartoum aerodrome is seen from the air shortly before Menzies was posted to No. 47 (B) Squadron. (Menzies family collection)

(Patrol S.8), including No. 47 (B) Squadron, in response. The objectives were to stop the unrest, capture the leaders and destroy the 'pyramid' at Guek's base, the village of Deng Kur. The pyramid was a large, conical mound, constructed largely of mud, which had been raised by Guek's father, the prophet Ngundeng. The pyramid was of significance to Guek's followers and destroying it would remove a potential future rallying point. Later, the pyramid was to be the scene of almost comical attempts at destruction, shrugging off bombs from the air and explosives set at the base before the army brutalised it enough to satisfy themselves.

Bombing and reconnaissance operations were carried out by the squadron in December 1927, and by the end of January 1928 it was considered that organised resistance had broken down and there were 'no real objectives for troops or aircraft'.[xii]

After the conclusion of those operations, No. 47 (B) Squadron's presence as a deterrent was emphasised with specific demonstrations, and a landing ground was established at Malakal from where future operations against Nuer tribes could conveniently be flown. Nevertheless, it appears that the squadron maintained a reasonably good relationship with the local peoples. According to Duncan's son Peter, he had a great admiration for the Sudanese he came into contact with.

Extreme weather could make life difficult. As Duncan was transferring from No. 45 Squadron, five of No. 47 (B) Squadron's machines were forced to land at Sinkat

Nuers from Southern Sudan, a people
Menzies admired greatly, though
No. 47 (B) Squadron was required to
bomb Nuer strongholds during periods of
unrest. (Menzies family collection)

during a flight to Port Sudan by a *haboob* (an intense dust storm carried on a weather front), and the following day the same aircraft, leaving Port Sudan, were forced to land at Jebel Sinei and again at Hedaliye by sandstorms.

At this time, No. 47 (B) Squadron was equipped with Fairey IIIF Mk I aircraft, which Duncan was by now familiar with due to his practice on SR1143 during his previous squadron's preparations to re-equip with the type. In fact, No. 47 (B) was the first squadron of any service to use the IIIF operationally, even though the ten development aircraft taken on charge in 1927 had actually been ordered by the Fleet Air Arm. For this reason, the first batch of IIIFs operated by No. 47 (B) Squadron were three-seaters built for the naval spotter-reconnaissance role rather than two-seater general purpose RAF-specification aircraft. Aircraft of the appropriate type (Mk IV C or Mk IV M) began to arrive from November 1928, and these steadily replaced the Mk Is as the earlier aircraft were returned to the depot for repair or overhaul. Like the DH.9A, the IIIF was straightforward to fly, robust and well-suited to operation in primitive conditions, while having significantly better performance. It was also rare for the time in having wing flaps, consisting of trailing edge flaps and drooping 'flaperons', operated by a crank in the pilot's cockpit, which altered the wing section to generate more lift. J. C. Nesbit-Dufort DSO described the IIIF as, 'A real old gentleman's aeroplane; rock steady, no vices and oh so easy to fly.'[xiii] It was capable of a maximum speed of around 150 mph at sea level,

One of the hazards of flying in desert areas was the likelihood of dust storms like this one in Sudan around 1929 – they could be lethal. (Menzies family collection)

or around 135 mph when fitted with float undercarriage. Ten days after Menzies arrived at the squadron, one of its aircraft was converted to floatplane configuration and was successfully launched on the Nile, though the experiment was not without difficulty. On 10 July, the current caught the starboard float as the aircraft was being hoisted out of the water with sufficient force that the aircraft was dragged under and sank. Later that day, though, another converted aircraft was successfully launched.

Unfortunately, Menzies' first days at his new squadron were affected by reliability problems with the Fairey aircraft. During a practice bombing sortie on 11 July, the release gear of J9153 broke, and two days later, on a flight to Jebel Aulia, he had to carry out a forced landing due to engine failure on S1145. This was part of a 'route proving' flight to El Obeid inspecting landing grounds at Dilling, Kedugli, Talodi, Soderi and Bare. Menzies was able to continue after repairs had been affected, and proceeded to El Obeid later that day, 'there,' states the squadron's Operations Record Book, 'completing another link of the direct route to Fasher'.

The rainy season arrived early in 1929, making life difficult and unpleasant for the squadron. 'Throughout the month bad weather prevailed, the aerodrome being partially under water for a considerable portion of the month,' described the squadron diary entry for 31 July. 'Rains were exceptionally heavy and a month before their usual date. The bombing range and targets were completely isolated.' On 15 August the diary added,

Menzies and fellow pilots and airmen of No. 47 (B) Squadron with one of the unit's Fairey IIIF Mk IV aircraft. Menzies is in the white overalls. (Menzies family collection)

'Heavy rain has made all the country around the aerodrome into a large lake. Consequently training (Bombing and Air Gunnery) has been delayed.' Menzies was charged with photographing the extent of the flood on the aerodrome, which he accomplished with a flight on the 13th, with a further flight to obtain overlapping photographs for a 'mosaic' on the 23rd.

With the difficulties on the aerodrome, it was perhaps not surprising that the squadron took the opportunity to undertake floatplane training on the White Nile on 28 August. After practising taxiing, Menzies was one of four pilots to successfully go solo on the floatplane IIIF.

John Nesbit-Dufort describes floatplane operation of the floatplane IIIF in his book *Open Cockpit*:

Take-off could be quite hard work. The procedure was as follows: first find a clear run of at least a mile, then, having turned into wind, complete the cockpit check, which included winding on a few degrees of camber, disengage the water rudders and open up [the throttle] fully ... The IIIF now ploughed along fussily at a speed of about 30 knots and would continue to do so indefinitely if no further action was taken, so the control column was pumped backwards and forward and this movement continued with decreasing violence until the rocking motion was sufficient to get the floats up on their 'steps'; when this occurred the controls were centralised. After a further quarter

Fairey IIIF floatplanes of No. 47 (B) Squadron on the Nile at Khartoum in 1929. Menzies' first experience of flying from water came during the squadron's periodical operation from the Nile. (Menzies family collection)

mile or so a gentle backward pressure on the stick resulted in one feeling a pronounced acceleration as she 'unstuck'.[xiv]

Landing, by contrast, was straightforward, as the floats enabled the aircraft to land in flying attitude, much as a tricycle undercarriage did. Operating in calm conditions added further difficulties, as it became virtually impossible to make the floats rise onto the steps unless a pilot was able to taxi across his own wake. When landing, if the water was too calm, it became very difficult to judge height.

Menzies, having never flown a floatplane before, did well by any objective standards to solo within a few hours' acquaintance.

After Menzies had been at No. 47 (B) Squadron for some months, a somewhat out-of-the-ordinary task was required of the squadron. Among the multifarious roles taken on by the RAF across the Empire in that era, a new one was helping the civilian authorities deal with the menace of locust infestations. The squadron diary describes the operation:

During this month aircraft were employed in the anti-locust campaign. Districts were visited and poison carried to the affected areas. The use of aircraft was in the nature of an experiment and proved of value, and it is the intention to draw up a comprehensive programme for the use of aircraft in the 1930 anti-locust campaign, i.e. for conveying personnel quickly from place to place. Collecting information from outstations where there is no telegraph etc.[xv]

Duncan's log book covering the period 6–8 September 1929 shows that he was heavily involved in this programme in the North-Eastern Kassala province, making five flights of up to 2 hours' duration on 6 August, four on 7 August and three on 8 August, criss-crossing the country from Khartoum to Jebel Geili, Abu Deleig, Kassala, Sarsareib and Wadi Hassunia. The log books state that he was 'co-operating with Governor of Kassala Province in Locust War' and refer to carrying 'poison for locusts' on 7 August on a flight from Kassala to Jebel Geili, and 'sacks of poison' on a similar flight on the following day. Menzies also transported 'native police' with the poison on 7 August, and recorded 'taking petrol to F/Lt Waite' on a flight from Kassala to Sarsareib on the same day. The very term 'Locust War' is descriptive of the desperate struggle against the crop-stripping insects that the province still suffers from to this day, and it was clearly an intensive period of flying. This cannot have been helped by a shortage of spares for the IIIF airframe and its Napier Lion XIA engine, noted at the end of the previous month, which 'handicapped serviceability of aircraft'.

In addition to the blight of locusts, the rains had not yet entirely given up their grip, and the squadron carried out more reconnaissance of flooded areas on 24 September. The Kassala railway line was damaged by the Rahad and Dindas rivers bursting their banks, and Menzies flew to the former river in IIIF SR1176, carrying two civilians, a Mr Graham and E. H. Nightingale, District Commissioner for the District of Darfur, to inspect the damage.

Various reconnaissance flights were made over this period. The authorities were concerned about the possibility of incursions from Ethiopia taking advantage of the British pacification of Eastern Sudan. Policy at the time involved the so-called 'Nuer Settlement', following the suppression of Guek Ngundeng, which was to restrict the Nuer tribes to their own territories and create a 'no man's land' between them and the Dinka peoples. As part of attempts to dissuade Ethiopian tribes from crossing the border, three chiefs from that country were taken on flights at the request of the government. Menzies undertook flights near the border, reconnoitring the 'Gallabat track', a route from Gederef (Al Qadarif) to the border village of Gallabat: he recorded that the grass on the track was 10–12 ft high (Sudanese grass can grow up to 15 ft high). In November Duncan flew a photographic reconnaissance to Shendi for the Director of Forests on the 13th, his passengers being LAC Ellis and a Mr Moore.

In December, Menzies finally got to take part in the Lloyd Cup long-distance 'reliability trial' – an inter-squadron endurance flying test. The route No. 47 Squadron had to fly was from Khartoum to Assuit and back. On the 2nd, Duncan flew Fairey IIIF Mk IV J9162, his passenger being LAC Williams, with the squadron from Khartoum to Atbara, 185 miles to the north, then 200 miles to Wadi Halfa on the northern border and to Aswan in Egypt, a flight of 185 miles. The following day saw a similar aerial marathon – 240 miles to Asyut (Assuit), then back to Atbara by the 4th, when a night flight to Shendi added some spice to the mix, arriving back at Khartoum on the 5th.

Unfortunately, the extensive night-flying practice had not prevented difficulties during the trial. The squadron's Operations Record Book entry reads: 'The third day the squadron carried out a night flight from Atbara to Shendi (90 miles). Two aircraft crashed on landing. Ten successfully completed the test arriving home on the 5th.' The squadron had not managed to win overall, but getting ten aircraft to the finish after 1,600 miles flying in four days could still be regarded as an achievement. A week afterwards, Menzies covered a similar route flying solo, carrying ballast on the outward journey, to escort His Excellency the High Commissioner of Sudan, Sir Percy Lorraine, and Air Vice-Marshal Scarlet, the Air Officer Commanding Middle East, from Wadi Halfa to Khartoum. Menzies carried the High Commissioner's Private Secretary, Mr Herbert, on the return flight.

The squadron's ceremonial duties were abruptly followed by the first military action Menzies had been involved with directly. On Christmas Eve 1929, the Sudan Defence Force (SDF) headquarters requested No. 47 (B) Squadron undertake offensive operations against the 'Nubas' of Jebel Eliri, in the Nuba Mountains of the Kordofan province. Patrol S.10 was formed and bombing missions commenced.

Mr F. Montague MP, Under Secretary of State for Air, when introducing the Air Estimates in the House of Commons in 1930 referred to these operations in his speech as an example of successful 'air control':

> Another recent illustration of the efficacy of air action occurred in the Sudan during December, 1929 where a small section of the Nuba tribe in Kordofan offered armed resistance to the police when engaged in the arrest of a certain head man who had defied the Government. The tribesmen took refuge in a strong natural position, and it became necessary to assemble a force of about 300 infantry to deal with them. The local Governor decided to induce surrender by taking air action in the first instance. After three days' bombing the position was occupied by the infantry without any casualties. There is no doubt that but for the preliminary air action undertaken the operation could not have been carried through without heavy loss of life on both sides.[xvi]

The operations actually took around a week. The entry in the squadron's Operations Record Book for 24 December reads: 'Air Operations against the NUBAS (Patrol S.10) were undertaken at the request of HQ SDF. By the 31st there were decided signs of the enemy giving in.'[xvii] The entry on 1 January 1930 reads: 'Further Reconnaissances and Bomb raids were carried out on January 1st and 2nd. January 3rd saw the collapse of Nuba Operations.'[xviii] Unfortunately, the appendices detailing the operations are missing from the squadron diary.

There is no evidence Menzies took part directly in bombing operations, and his log books do not indicate any offensive actions. He did assist with reconnaissance, however, and on 28–29 December he flew the Staff Officer, Colonel Wilson, to observe the scene of operations four times between El Obeid and Tolodi.

It is possible, however, that he did take part in offensive action. A family friend, Chris Howard, recounts a conversation with Duncan, writing: 'I remember he told me about one occasion when his Commanding Officer detailed him to drop a bomb (hand delivered over the side) on a village that had been causing problems.' The most likely occasion for this action was the operation against the Nuba between December 1929 and

January 1930. It is also not quite true that the operations were completed without any casualties – on 3 December, an unexploded 112 lb bomb from one of the raids against the Nuba at Jebel Eliri was discovered by a Sudanese who brought it towards a party of RAF and SDF. The bomb exploded, killing three Sudanese soldiers and wounding Dr Hall of the SDF Medical Services, the District Commissioner Mr Oakley, and LAC Prust, who had flown with Duncan on numerous occasions. Menzies had been there the day before.

The new year of 1933 got going with a cross-country flight to Egypt in IIIF J9140, A. C. Thompson in the back seat, tracing the course of the Nile north, from Khartoum to Atbara, Atbara to Wadi Halfa, Aswan, Asyut, Helwan, and Aboukir. Menzies plotted out the distance on the back page of his first log book, the stage and final distances marked in red ink. Aboukir is 1,237 miles from Khartoum. The time in the air was 11 hours 40 minutes. There, the Fairey probably had its engine replaced or overhauled. An engine test on the 14th and it was straight back the next day. This time the stages were longer, with no stop at Aswan, and flying time was a brisk 8 hours and 50 minutes. Perhaps he had the nod from his CO to make a rapid transit, or perhaps he got lucky with a good tailwind, but either way he set a new speed record.

The *Northern Times* briefly recorded the feat, which otherwise seems to have been overlooked: 'A new aviation speed record was set up by Flying Officer Duncan Menzies when he flew from Aboukir in Egypt to Khartoum, the capital of Sudan – a journey of 1,267 miles – in 8 hours 50 minutes in a Fairey IIIF biplane. Duncan was the son of Mr James Menzies, Rogart.'[xix]

In those days records fell all the time – it was part of Trenchard's vision for the peacetime RAF to keep itself in the public eye. By early 1930 the point-to-point records set by service pilots were less glamorous and less accessible to the public than the outright speed records and Schneider Trophy win witnessed by thousands off the south coast of England the previous year. Perhaps long-distance flights were becoming more associated with romantic civilian adventurers, the Freddie Guests and Tom Campbell Blacks. These were characters Menzies would have been all too familiar with, given the frequency their Moths and Fokkers staged through Khartoum on record-setting or route-proving flights. Perhaps it was just Menzies' characteristic modesty that led to a distinct lack of fanfare over the feat.

One of these civilian adventurers was Count Collobiano, an Italian aviator who went missing on a flight from Rome to Capetown in March, after having used No. 47 Squadron's landing ground at Malakal. The squadron scoured the wilderness for the Count without success, and two of the three search aircraft had to force-land at Bor, one of them being totally wrecked. The Count eventually turned up at Khartoum, having crashed at Yambio and taken the steamer from Juba. The squadron's opinion of him is not recorded.

A break from the usual duties was provided with the air display at Heliopolis, which must have provided a welcome relief for No. 47 (B) Squadron. Nine of its aircraft participated in three events, formation manoeuvres and the massed fly-past (both of which Menzies took part in), and the 'spot landing' contest, which was won by the squadron's Flight Lieutenant Waite.

Meanwhile, the occasion that was to be the culmination of Menzies' early RAF career approached. The heir to the throne of the United Kingdom, Edward, Prince of Wales, was then engaged in an ambitious two-month safari, run for him by another of those adventurers who had made Africa their home and playground – Denys Finch Hatton, later immortalised as the romantic hero in *Out of Africa*. Finch Hatton edged the Prince towards filming and photography of game rather than shooting it, and as a result the 1930 royal safari today holds a particular significance in the beginning of environmental consciousness.[xx] The royal party made its languid progress through Kenya, Tanganyika, Uganda and Congo, towards Sudan.

The preparations for the arrival of the royal party at Khartoum were in hand, and No. 47 Squadron's aircraft spent the middle of March darting about landing grounds, checking they were in good order, measuring fuel consumption from point-to-point. The flights were partly justified as 'showing our flag' in the squadron diary. Menzies headed north and west, undertaking photography. Destinations included Gebeit (Jubayt), Port Sudan, Kassala. The flights took in Suakin, which is singled out for special attention in Menzies's log book.

There was yet more formation training at the end of that month, and it is hard to escape the suspicion that this stemmed from a desire to impress the Prince. Further excitement arose when Menzies made a test flight on the 1st to 15,500 ft in IIIF SR1172, flying into a snowstorm at 14,000 ft – it wouldn't be his last encounter with such conditions. On the 3rd, the Prince, his entourage and Finch Hatton arrived.

The ancient port of Suakin in North-West Sudan, on an inlet of the Red Sea. Menzies flew photographic sorties over Suakin during his posting to No. 47 (B) Squadron. (Menzies family collection)

Denys Finch Hatton had developed a great enthusiasm for flying and was at the time pioneering game reconnaissance from the air. He had learned to fly and later bought an example of the ubiquitous de Havilland Moth, made famous by the likes of Amy Johnson and Tom Campbell Black (who was actually involved in the safari too, having been engaged by Finch Hatton to organise the delivery of supplies by air). Fortunately for Finch Hatton, the Prince was in a position to engage No. 47(B) Squadron to assist in the safari. He held the rank of Group Captain in the RAF and was just as enthusiastic about flying as his hunting. If there was any sense in the squadron that acting as a taxi service for the heir to the throne was not the business of a frontline bomber squadron, it has not survived. More likely, of course, is that providing that service to the Prince was the source of pride.

Menzies' first contact with the royal party was on 3 April 1930, when he flew 'Mails for HRH the Prince of Wales' between Malakal and Juba. The following day, Menzies took Finch Hatton up in Fairey IIIF J9156 on a 'game recco' and escort to the Prince, between Mongalla and Juba. Over the next few days, Menzies criss-crossed the Southern Sudanese landscape between Juba, Mongalla, Torit and Yei, inspecting suitable landing grounds for the safari. 'In the sudd they steamed along torpid creeks lined with hippo landing stages, and the prince, who was experimenting with colour film, photographed Nile lechwe, the semi-amphibious antelope that live only in Southern Sudan,' wrote Sara Wheeler in her biography of Finch Hatton, *Too Close To The Sun*.[xxi]

Menzies flew Finch Hatton again after a week, when the squadron took the Prince and his whole party from Malakal to Kosti on the White Nile, where they stopped to refuel, before heading on to Khartoum. A few days after that, over 16–17 April, the squadron, with Menzies once again acting as chauffeur to Finch Hatton, flew north, out of Sudan and back to Heliopolis in Egypt – not quite out of Africa, but to its edge.

Altogether, Duncan flew Finch Hatton for more than 16 hours over those two weeks, yet sadly no indication survives in letters, anecdotes or family legends of what kind of relationship they might have built up over that time. Did Finch Hatton know that he was being flown from Khartoum to Cairo by the current record holder for that route? Did flying with Menzies further stoke his passion for aviation? Unfortunately, the answers to such questions are lost in time. Sara Wheeler notes that after the party was transported by RAF aircraft, 'They all boarded the S.S. *Rawalpindi* – Denys was returning to England with the royals. He was determined to buy his plane.' So perhaps it is not stretching a point to suggest that the experience had provided a spur.

Also travelling with the royal party and Finch Hatton aboard the P&O steamer SS *Rawalpindi* was one Flying Officer D. Menzies, RAF. Menzies' tour in the Middle East was over – in fact, his return had been delayed so he could assist the Prince's safari – and after seeing the party safely to Cairo, he took a ship for the UK, but his accommodation was as one of the 290 second-class passengers rather than the 310 first-class that included the royal party.

Chapter 5

Back to the UK, 1930

Duncan Menzies, in cabin 352 off the second-class saloon, was not to be completely separated from the Royals by barriers of status. Peter, the younger of Duncan's two sons, recalls what happened on the voyage home:

> The Prince learned that my father had delayed his leave and that he was returning home on the same ship, and invited him to dinner one night – I still have the invitation. The RAF personnel were all berthed 'below the waterline,' and the stewards would turn them away from the 1st Class bars. When he went to dinner with the Prince, the stewards tried to turn him back!

Fortunately, Menzies was able to persuade the stewards that he had an appointment with the Prince.

A note delivered to Menzies' cabin signed P. W. Legh (Captain the Honourable Piers W. Legh, Equerry to the Prince of Wales) on 24 April, stated simply: 'Dear Menzies, The Prince is not changing for dinner to-night.' Peter believes this was a gesture on behalf of the Prince to ensure Duncan was not made to feel uncomfortable by his lack of formal attire. It's the sort of personal touch that not only emphasises just how rigid class structures and social proprieties were at the time, but also how a simple relaxation of the code could bridge the divide. Peter said that Duncan had later recalled that the Prince was 'absolutely charming'. He continues:

> The Prince of Wales was very interested in what the life of a young Air Force officer was. He questioned my father quite closely, because he was a modern young man. My father said, 'Well, I love it but I'm a bit fed up. I've been in the Air Force for donkey's years and I've only flown two or three types of aircraft.' The Prince of Wales said to him, 'What would you have to do to fly more different types of aircraft?' And Dad said, 'I'd have to get a posting to Martlesham Heath, and be able to start test-flying.'

Martlesham Heath was then the home of the Aeroplane & Armament Experimental Establishment, and the very word 'Martlesham' was synonymous with test-flying. The Prince made no overt offers of help, and nothing more was said about a career in test-flying; however, in later years Menzies would often wonder if the Prince had taken a more direct interest in, and influence over, his career, though he probably thought little more about it at the time. While Menzies remained aboard the *Rawalpindi*, the Prince disembarked at Marseilles where once again he was able to take advantage of the RAF to fly him home. The Prince's return from Sudan was covered by *Flight*, which reported the following in the 2 May 1930 issue:

H.R.H. the Prince of Wales arrived home from Africa on April 25, when he landed on his private aerodrome in Windsor Great Park. Quite a considerable portion of the Prince's journey home has been carried out by air. The Prince and his party left Malakal on April 13 in RAF Fairey IIIF machines and flew to Khartoum, via Kosti. The journey was continued on April 16 to Wadi Haifa and Assuan [Aswan], and Cairo was reached the following day.

The Prince proceeded by the P. and O. liner *Rawalpindi* to Marseilles, where he arrived on April 25 at 5.45 a.m. Meanwhile, three RAF machines—one a Westland 'Wapiti' piloted by Sqn Ldr Don, and the others, a Fairey IIIF piloted by Flight-Lieut. A. W. Heslop and another 'Wapiti' piloted by Flying Officer H. W. Pearson-Rogers set out from Northolt on April 22 for Marseilles, where they arrived on April 24, for it was announced that, weather permitting, the Prince would make the last stage of the journey home by air.

Thus, immediately the *Rawalpindi* docked, the Prince, who wore a light grey suit with a grey-blue pull-over, and his party motored to the Marignane aerodrome, where the three RAF machines were in readiness. At 7.35 a.m. the three machines started off, the Prince in the 'Wapiti' piloted by Sqn Ld. Don.[xxii]

It would take Menzies several more weeks to reach Britain aboard the *Rawalpindi*. Whether or not anything further would arise from the conversation with the Prince, Menzies had in any event marked himself out as among the cream of the crop. On returning to the UK, Menzies was posted to the Central Flying School at Wittering to train as a flying instructor – a task generally reserved for the best pilots.

The Prince of Wales (the future Edward VIII) climbing out of an RAF biplane on his return to England after safari where No. 47 (B) Squadron provided the transport. Menzies dined with the Prince on the P&O steamer *Rawalpindi* before the latter disembarked to fly home. (Author's collection)

He arrived at Wittering on 20 May 1930 and immediately began the rigorous advanced training that would enable him to teach tyro pilots. The course involved forced landing practice, learning more about the effects of the controls, aerobatics, spinning and so on. During the course he flew Avro 504s, Bristol F2Bs and his first single-seat fighter, an Armstrong-Whitworth Siskin.

The course was, as might be expected, intense – three or four flights every day through May, June, July, etc., and included solo spinning, aerobatics, inverted flying, cross-country flights to Duxford, Manston, Cranwell. On 15 July he underwent a test at the hands of Squadron Leader Whistler, the officer in charge of the Flying School. Two weeks later, Menzies participated in the Clarkson Trophy for inter-flight aerobatics. The course seems to have rekindled Menzies' enthusiasm for the discipline, or perhaps it never left, opportunities for aerobatting being thin in bomber squadrons.

On 1 August, Duncan was rated 'exceptional' at the CFS – a rare accolade and further indication that Menzies was among the best of his peers. Then, after just three months in the UK following three years overseas, Menzies was bound for the Middle East again.

Duncan's year at the Central Flying School, RAF Wittering, 1930. Menzies is standing sixth from the left in the second row from the back. (Menzies family collection)

Chapter 6

'Exceptional': Instructor
4 FTS, 1930–32

Menzies' first posting after graduating as an instructor was as a glorified aerial taxi driver at the Communication Flight, Station Headquarters, Heliopolis. This was just a temporary measure and he would be there for less than two weeks. The flights ranged from ten-minute hops from Abu Sueir to Moascar by the Canal to long-distance flights ferrying officers to far-flung postings. Kolundia in Gaza, Amman in Transjordan ... Marathon flights across the vast empty spaces of the Empire were becoming routine to Duncan. Or perhaps such flights are never routine: a single biplane tracing its lonely path over desert, sand giving way to rock or earth, occasionally slashed by vehicle tracks, or not, the sun burning off the polished cowlings, the pilot monitoring the instruments, listening to the Napier Lion for problems.

There was time for one solo aerobatics flight.

While at the Communications Flight was again rated 'above the average'. In October, Menzies was posted back to 4 FTS, where his RAF career had begun, this time as an instructor with 'B' Flight, the *ab initio* unit. The Avros were newer radial-engined 'N' models rather than the rotary-engined 'K's – presumably Duncan never had to fine a student for blipping a Monosoupape.

It was straight to business. On the 8th, flights in Avro J8720 with three students – medium and steep turns, landings and take-offs – then four students the next day and three the day after. Most of October, November and December passed thus, bar the odd flight in a Ninak or Fairey or Atlas for different purposes, service training, or just travelling from one aerodrome to another.

Menzies had by now developed a flair for aerobatics, and in addition to his duties as an instructor with 'B' Flight, some of his time at Abu Sueir during the winter months was spent in honing this skill. While the Avro 504N was an ideal basic training aircraft, it was also capable, in the right hands, of an impressive display. In February 1931 Duncan began preparations for a 'crazy flying' routine in the RAF display to be held at Heliopolis, in amongst flights with students.

It was here that Duncan would meet a friend for life in Humphrey Edwardes-Jones, known to all as E. J. He was one of only a few of Duncan's RAF friends and acquaintances to survive the Second World War. There are photographs from that time of Duncan and E. J. out and about in Cairo in their suits and broad-brimmed hats, showing the sights to E. J.'s two sisters.

Duncan flew to Heliopolis on 16 February, where three days were devoted to practising in Avro J8534 before the display itself. An air-to-air photo taken at this time shows three Avro Lynx biplanes above the aerodrome. They hold a very close 'vic' formation, with the wings of the two trailing aircraft tucked tightly behind those of the leading aircraft. And, almost incidentally, the leading aircraft is flying inverted. It demonstrates the incredible skill of these pilots, who were enjoying themselves but were thoroughly professional in the 'finest flying club in the world'. Menzies' performance was evidently popular as he repeated it at the following year's RAF Air Display at Heliopolis, and in May at Geziro for Empire Day.

But the majority of the work was training pilots. While Duncan's log books had previously been devoted entirely to himself and his own flights, now they started to include notes on student pilots. Intriguingly, one of Duncan's student at this point is an officer with the rank of Squadron Leader, who it seems was in dire need of a refresher course on his flying. Perhaps he had held a desk job for a while, or been ill, or had even been studying medicine – a medical paper about a serious bacterial infection written by that officer appeared in a prominent journal in 1940. He held a rather prestigious decoration, so it's hard to imagine his flying was always as bad as it is described in Menzies' log book. 'Holding too much bank,' was the diagnosis on 12 May, and the following day, 'Gliding turns bad. Holding off bank.' At this point, Menzies stops writing in neat block capitals. All his notes on the Squadron Leader are written in tight cursive script as if Duncan was concerned the senior officer was peering over his shoulder at the entries. By the 15th, the officer's turns are better, and he was 'showing some confidence'. This was probably just as well, as the next time Menzies flew with him, it was to practise 'loops' and 'slow rolls'.

Three Avro 504Ns performing formation aerobatics in February 1931 during Menzies' preparations for his 'crazy flying' display at Heliopolis. (Menzies family collection)

After this, and probably coming as a blessed relief, was four days' solo flying Armstrong Whitworth (AW) Atlas K1474 to prepare for the Empire Day air display. The next entry detailing the Squadron Leader's refresher course is written in such tight, dense script that it is illegible. The next is readable, but does not make good reading – 'Still skidding in turns.' A few days later though, evolutions are 'accurate and confident', and apart from one further flight on 2 June in a Bristol Fighter, that was the last the log books see of the Squadron Leader. The senior officer's RAF career continued, with him rising through the ranks, so it can safely be surmised that he passed whatever requirements were placed on him.

After that, Duncan moved almost wholesale from flying Avros to the larger AW Atlas, having switched to 'A' Flight. The Atlas belonged to the same stable as the AW Siskin Duncan had flown at Wittering, and resembled it in its general form – a distinctly unequal, almost sesquiplane layout to the wings with a large, broad-chord upper plane almost double the size of the lower and a chunky fuselage with an Armstrong-Siddeley Jaguar fourteen-cylinder radial engine attached awkwardly to the nose. The Atlas was developed to replace the DH.9A in the 'army co-operation' category, a range of battlefield roles such as tactical reconnaissance and close support. Menzie's role had effectively changed too. No longer would he teach pilots how to fly an aeroplane so much as how to use that aeroplane for a specific task.

In October of 1931, a vision of modernity descended on Abu Sueir in the form of K1991, the second experimental Fairey Long Range Monoplane, on a proving flight to Abu Sueir ahead of its distance record attempt. Menzies took a keen interest in the machine when it visited Egypt. He was photographed with it, standing by the rear fuselage. It must have seemed a glimpse into the future, sitting on the apron with the boxy biplanes. Even Tom Campbell Black's Avro 619 monoplane, which had staged through Khartoum when Duncan was with No. 47 (B) Squadron, had not the streamlined sleekness, the simplicity of outline and purpose as K1991. The Fairey's thick cantilever wing was self-supporting, with no ugly bracing to interfere with the airflow apart from a few streamlined struts for the undercarriage. The mainplane was tapered from the rounded tips to the broad roots, spreading from the fuselage like muscular shoulders. Even the main wheels were sheltered from the airflow with teardrop-shaped spats. The fuselage was a slender tube of oval section and within it more futuristic wonders resided, in the shape of an automatic pilot.

The sight was edged with danger as well – the first Long Range Monoplane had flown into a mountain as it attempted the world distance record in 1929. The second Monoplane would make its own flight, from Cranwell to Walvis Bay, South-West Africa, in February 1933, covering 5,410 miles, winning the record.

It is stimulating to imagine the thoughts of the RAF officer, who in late 1931 had already set his heart on test-flying, casting his eye over a machine built by an organisation he would later test-fly hundreds of aeroplanes for, none of them as purely experimental as the Long Range Monoplane, but just as cutting-edge in their way, and several of which could trace their design lineage from it.

But this is all still in the future. In the here and now there is plenty to keep Duncan occupied, with his duties and a spot of stunting to leaven the serious training.

It's obvious from Duncan's log books that aerobatics were something he took pride and probably pleasure in. Rarely does a page go by without at least one aerobatic flight wedged in amongst the trips with students. This is not to say that he didn't take his

Above: In October 1931, Fairey Long Range Monoplane K1991 flew to Abu Sueir on a practice flight for an attempt on the long distance record. Menzies inspected the aircraft during its visit. (Author's collection)

Left: Menzies with the Fairey Long Range Monoplane K1991. This machine secured the long distance record in a flight from Cranwell to Walvis Bay in early 1933. (Menzies family collection)

main task seriously – he clearly did, and his Commanding Officer thought so too, if the proficiency ratings Menzies received from 4 FTS are any guide. But his skill as an aerobatic pilot, particularly in the jaunty 'crazy flying' routine, were also prized. Five days of January 1932 were set aside for practice. The flying may have been crazy, but it would have been insane not to prepare thoroughly.

Air displays, it seems, were a way in which the usually retiring Menzies could enable his flying to do the talking – almost literally, according to an effusive newspaper report of his performance at Heliopolis on 12 February, 1932. The *Egyptian Gazette* wrote:

> The most popular event on the programme was crazy flying by Flight Lieutenant F. K. Damant and Flying Officer D. Menzies, in Avro Lynxes. These two pilots did everything with their machines except make them talk. It was amazing to see what a 'plane could stand. Evolutions which looked as though they must snap the machine in half were carried out again and again. The skill of these two pilots was almost uncanny; they seemed almost part of their 'planes, and the 'planes were nearly human in the way they responded to the controlling hand. At one time the 'planes did kind of [a] little dance along the ground in front of the spectators.

It's an eye-opening glimpse into a pre-war aerobatic display. One wonders what Menzies or Damant could achieve with a modern carbon-fibre Sukhoi or Extra today.

Menzies with sergeants and airmen pose with an Avro 504N in Egypt in 1930. Menzies became adept at aerobatics in this type, with an admired display of 'crazy flying'. (Menzies family collection)

And then, the fun over, came the inevitable return to training students.

The territory exacted a price too. On 22 February, a big, twin-engined Vickers Victoria went missing. Once again there was a search. Menzies flew for 45 minutes with LAC Whelan in the back of his Atlas, searching. The results of the search aren't clear, but no fatalities are recorded from the loss of a Victoria on that date, so it seems reasonable to conclude that the crew were found and survived. Not without irony, Duncan's very next flights were participation in 4 FTS' 'Forced Landing Competition'. It was at least a practice that the RAF took seriously, and training, until it became second nature, saved lives. It would save Duncan's more than once in the years to come.

There were other dangers besides getting lost. Menzies, now commanding 'C' Flight, was landing Atlas K1473 at the aerodrome on 4 May after a solo test flight when two LACs in K1192 contrived to collide with it. The aircraft was a write-off. Duncan's thoughts on the two men are unrecorded, but one of them was one of his students, flying with him every other day, and some time later the other was subjected to a progress test by Menzies. How it must have felt to train with an instructor whose aircraft they had wrecked, the Commanding Officer of their course, is an intriguing thought.

The 'C' Flight course Duncan was leading progressed through its basic service training throughout the spring of 1932. One by one, the pilots went solo on the Atlas. As spring gave way to summer, training evolved to formation flying, navigating in cloud and point-to-point flights in formation.

This was all leading up to the culmination of the course, which would be an adventure in its own right – a formation flight to Diana in Mesopotamia ('Mespot' to the British) and back: almost 2,000 miles of flying. The Atlases would cross a vast swathe of territory, and four countries, Egypt, Palestine, Transjordan, and, finally, Iraq. The flight would serve training purposes, of course, but it was also the Empire testing its reach and exercising its muscles.

Iraq was the main laboratory for air power as a tool of Imperial control. The Middle Eastern territories Britain had secured from the break-up of the Ottoman Empire promised to enrich and impoverish at the same time. The resources there made Iraq worth hanging on to (under its League of Nations mandate), even at the cost of reneging on previous promises of autonomy, first to the Arabs and then the Kurds, even after a revolt in 1920.[6] But the cost of garrisoning when the war-weary British public expected a peace dividend was not tenable. The answer, as in Somalia, was 'air control'. The Iraq Levies, British-officered local troops (mostly Assyrian), were formed while eight RAF squadrons, some supporting armoured car units and a few British and Indian infantry battalions, were transferred to Iraq.

These forces could expect to prevail in the case of localised uprisings or small-scale incursions over the border. The feeling was that bombing the natives from the air would scare them into submission. It worked, after a fashion, though it was far from the panacea the regional commanders thought it to be and if a nationwide revolt broke out, or Turkey made good on threats to launch a full-scale invasion, urgent reinforcement would be needed. That was where the RAF in Egypt – and flights such as the one Duncan and his students were about to embark on – came in. The air bridge, over 1,000 miles of hostile country, could bring troops, heavy bombers and Atlases to support the Levies.

The air route from Cairo to Baghdad was one of the key early achievements of Trenchard's post-war policy. It was the primary means of reinforcing forces stationed in

'Mespot'. It has been likened to an aerial Suez Canal, with good reason. It was the sole means by which competing Imperial priorities could be balanced. The empty spaces on the map were being overlaid not just with Imperial writ but technology, in the all-metal aeroplanes able to cross continents as long as there was fuel for their 500 hp engines, and now invisibly in radio waves from their wireless telegraphy gear. This was no mere jaunt. The danger in the territory was real and could be deadly – spaces where no rescue could be made from the air, a bone-dry plateau that rose to 2,000 feet above sea level, mountains that could snare an unwary pilot in poor visibility or at night. The Bedouin, awash with rifles from the Arab revolt in the First World War, had no hesitation in taking pot-shots at any passing aircraft.

On 24 August 1932, five Atlases took off from Abu Sueir and swung onto an easterly course, crossing the Nile and heading over the Arabian Desert. Duncan was piloting Atlas Mk I K1016, with LAC Spring accompanying. The first leg was to take them to Ramleh (Ramla) in Palestine, 2 hours and 15 minutes away. There they refuelled, and flew on, taking 45 minutes to reach Amman, the capital of the Emirate of Transjordan, where they spent the night. Now they would truly be pushing out into the wilderness, with Amman the last glimpse of civilisation until Baghdad, nearly 500 miles away.

The next morning, the 'C' Flight course took off for Landing Ground 'D', one of two airfields scraped out of the desert on the Cairo–Baghdad route for aircraft to refuel in the

The epic training flight from Egypt to Iraq, which Menzies led with 'C' Flight, 4 FTS, in the late summer of 1932. Here the Atlases, with Menzies' aircraft K1016 leading, skirt hills between Barzan and Anadia. (Menzies family collection)

vast spaces between aerodromes. There were numerous temporary landing grounds but 'D' and 'V' were the only ones that had permanent fuel dumps. Any aircraft running out of petrol between those sites would be stuck until land vehicles reached them.

The next stage was a 2-hour leg to Rutbah, an old fort with a well that had been transformed into a rest stop. Before reaching the site the aircraft had to cross the vast Transjordan lava field, where no aircraft could land safely and not even the Bedouin saw any good reason to go. Even with wireless telegraphy, the chances of a crew coming down there were not favourable. The lava field formed a vast barrier of uneven black rock from the time it spewed across the Transjordan, in some primeval convulsion of the earth, until a road was finally bulldozed through it during the Second World War.

Rutbah was barely more established than Landing Ground 'D' in 1932. A photograph in Menzies' collection shows the almost comically small square of the fort, tents and a pale track slashing across the landscape in tiny and temporary incursions onto the vast plain surrounding it. From Rutbah, the Atlases continued, 55 minutes to Landing Ground 'V', refuel, then 2 hours to Hinaidi, just east of Baghdad.

They rested at Hinaidi on the 26th then proceeded – 2 hours to Kirkuk, and the following day on to Mosul. Another overnight stop, then to Diana in Kurdistan, nestling in the mountain ridges that skirt the north-west edge of Iraq, just 10 miles from the border with Persia.

The sheer distance covered can be seen with the maps used for this trip, a few of which Duncan kept. The ribbon of country between capitals was charted by long, thin sheets, approximately 3 ft x 8 in. The map covers the course from El Jid, just inside Iraq, to Baghdad. The route to fly – the only route – is marked in red, point-to-point between landing grounds. Alongside each leg are printed compass bearings and the distance, repeated in the opposite direction so the aviator can follow the map from each end. Weaving gently around the red line, in dark blue is 'the furrow' – a track marked out by vehicles in the early 1920s to provide 'Bradshaw' navigation through the wilderness ('Bradshawing' was the practice of navigating by railway lines). It would be difficult to think of anything more British than creating a false railway line through the desert for the Empire's aviators to follow.[xxiii]

Each stretch of 'the furrow' indicates the distance by car, and a description of the driveability – IX to 8 (probably for reasons of clarity, '8' is written in Arabic numerals while all the other landing grounds are rendered in Roman) 'going bumpy in places'. V to IV is 'very good going'. The terrain is described as 'open plain, covered with loam and small limestones', or 'rather broken country'. There is a table of distances in the bottom right corner, some of which Duncan has transferred in pencil to the appropriate part of the route.

The map is the third sheet the flight would have needed from Cairo, and at least one more would be required to get them to Diana. A conventional map of the Baghdad area from the era reveals how useless such a map was for aviators. Most of the area would be wasted. The few air routes might as well have been railway lines. To diverge from them would be unthinkable and to map the intervening ground pointless.

And yet, in this vast Empire, it was still a small world. Duncan's wife, years later, wrote on the reverse of a photograph taken during this trip, 'They breakfasted here at Diana in the Kurdistan Hills with a company of the Iraq Levies – the C.O. of which turned out to be the father of two boys who were at Alton Burn with him.'

'C' Flight landed at Diana in Kurdistan, where the local detachment of Iraq Levies happened to be led by Captain McKewan, the father of two boys Menzies went to school with. (Menzies family collection)

There are two photographs of that meeting, showing the pilots in their solar topees and shorts posing in front of the line of Atlases. They are relaxed after their long flight, glad to be out of the cockpit for a while. They flank Captain McKewan of the Levies, immaculate in his jodhpurs and 'slouch hat' with its plume.

The return route was a little different. Instead of flying directly to Mosul, the Atlases stopped at Barzan and Amadia (Al Amadiya).

Menzies kept some photographs from that trip – one of the men evidently had a decent camera, a Leica perhaps, certainly no Box Brownie, and knew how to use it. One air-to-air shot, taken between Barzan and Amadia, shows four Atlases in formation, Duncan's aircraft leading, from a fifth aircraft, framed against a crinkled mountain flank. It is quite extraordinarily evocative.

On the leg back to Kirkuk, on 30 August 1932, Duncan swapped passengers with LAC Senior now in the back seat. Then, 40 minutes in, the first trouble of the whole flight hit; a forced landing 10 minutes south-east of Mungub – was it engine failure? The log books do not say.

The terrain was flat, scattered with small stones but OK to put down on in a pinch. Test pilots who have made forced landings speak as if time slows down. A cascade of decisions and consequences stretch out before them; they take a route and follow it until circumstances change, then follow another branch. Has the engine failed completely or just lost power? Do the controls answer? Do we need to bail out? Call a quick warning to LAC Senior, tell him to signal over the W/T that we're making a forced landing. Eyes scanning for a suitable landing site. The rush of the wind where before there was nothing but the growl of the engine. Can we make LG 'V'? No. All looks fine below – a glimpse at the map strapped to the thigh to confirm. 'Level Plain.' Good. Nose down to keep up air speed, turn gently into wind. And then it's just like any landing at Abu Sueir. Put it down on the mainwheels – plenty of space to roll and no need to risk a three-pointer. Bit bumpy but could be worse ... hope the tyres hold on these stones. OK, it'll be all right.

Someone took the time to snap a few photographs. One shows pilots and back-seaters sitting around in a knot by the tail of Duncan's Atlas with an unidentified Iraqi in robes turning to look at the camera with suspicion, or possibly amusement. Duncan is smiling, even relaxed. A wireless set sits behind Duncan. It probably needed to be removed to allow the mechanic access to whatever went wrong. There is no danger of being swallowed up by the desert today.

The aircraft repaired, the flight continued to Kirkuk and then to Hinaidi where the five Atlases stopped for the night. There was another slight variation on the itinerary this time, with a stop at Romadi (Ramadi) on the Euphrates.

Menzies (on the left) was compelled to force-land his Atlas between Amadia and Kirkuk. The party, and a single Kurd, are seen here presumably waiting for repairs to be completed. (Menzies family collection)

An hour and a half into the leg to Rutbah, trouble hit again. They were forced down by a dust storm at Landing Ground III – the closest places marked on the map being two old ruined forts, Kasr Khubaz and Kasr Amej, only one of which had water. The map makes them look close to the landing ground. In reality they were 12 hours' walk from it, and each other. Duncan had photographs of a dust storm from this part of his career. They are remarkable phenomenon – a solid, opaque wall rising into the sky. Flying into one would not end well. Strong winds hide within them; the fine dust gets into engines and turns the lubricant to glue. Even today, dust storms can be deadly for aircraft.

'C' Flight rode out the storm at Landing Ground 'III', then returned to Romadi, with trouble in the wireless equipment. It was fixed, and Duncan carried out a quick W/T test flight at Romadi before heading off. This time they managed the 2-hour 25-minute flight to Rutbah without difficulty.

The remainder of the flight passed without incident, and the five aircraft were back at Abu Suier on 2 September.

In the meantime, modernity kept up its march. Science meant the British Empire would no longer have to draw railway lines across the landscape – instruments could now follow invisible railways in the sky, and pilots had to learn to read the runes – especially those entrusted with teaching others. In September, Duncan enrolled in the 1st Instrument Course at 4 FTS. Some Avro 504s had been modified with a hood over the rear cockpit to enable pilots to train with no external view at all, relying instead on the instruments in the cockpit. Menzies had flown at night, of course, but how different must this have been? Dave Gledhill, an RAF fast jet pilot in the 1980s, remarked that flying under the instrument hood, 'Blew my mind for the first time when I did my private flying.' He added: 'Hoods were only ever used with a safety pilot on board so no real utility for real. It was merely a way of ensuring that the pilot under training didn't peek. As we always said, a peep is worth a thousand sweeps!'[xxiv] This was also true of Duncan's training – at no point was he solo under instrument hood. The second pilot could always have taken control. Even so, the hour-long cross-country instrument flight on 21 September must have been a rare trial.

It was the first time in his flying career that Duncan did not take to a discipline naturally. It wasn't that he was bad at it – his proficiency was rated as 'average' – but it was the first (and last) time in his career that the box to record 'any special faults in flying which must be watched' had been used; the FTS's Commanding Officer wrote in it, 'Qualities as an instructor in instrument flying.'

After that course, Duncan continued instructing pilots with 'C' Flight. It was a busy period. Most days in October and November he was flying five or six times. On 1 November his log book lists nine flights, with four different students; on the 14th, just one – a 2-hour solo in an Avro that took him 140 miles across the Nile Delta from Abu Sueir to Aboukir, by way of a farewell to the Middle Eastern sky. He had been posted home. On 16 November 1932, Menzies was once again rated 'exceptional' by the Group Captain commanding 4 FTS, and in that 'special faults' box, a satisfactory 'nil'.

Part 2

Defence of the Realm

It is a strange and wonder-filled time. A glorious time. I am no longer fighting alone, but fighting with my airplane. And in the middle of a fight, a lesson. As long as the pilot can believe in his fight, and battle on, his airplane will battle with him.

Richard Bach

Chapter 7

Test Pilot, A&AEE, 1932–35

At the end of 1932, all Duncan's Christmases came at once: a posting as test pilot with the Aeroplane & Armament Experimental Establishment (A&AEE) at Martlesham Heath – exactly as he had suggested to the Prince of Wales two years previously.

Had the Prince taken an interest in his career? Perhaps had a quiet word in a few ears at the Air Ministry? It might just have been coincidence, of course. Plenty of pilots went to Martlesham without Royal patronage. Duncan would never find out.

On returning to England, he went to the Home Aircraft Depot at Henlow, where the RAF's engineering school was located, to bolster his technical knowledge before becoming a test pilot. He was also promoted to the rank of Flight Lieutenant (equivalent to a Captain in the Army or a Lieutenant in the Royal Navy).

In the early 1930s, Martlesham was the centre of the test-flying world. Every landplane[7] proposed for British military service went there for exhaustive assessment of its performance and handling, and new civilian aircraft were tested there for their Certificates of Airworthiness. The Air Ministry would also occasionally send examples of foreign aircraft with some feature of interest, to see what lessons might be gleaned for UK manufacturers.

Aviation was changing rapidly. The 'Ten Year' rule, which had become a 'rolling' rule at the behest of Winston Churchill, was finally abolished in March 1932. Even with the financial pressures of the Great Depression, the need to modernise and expand the RAF was recognised. Group Captain A. C. Maund, the officer commanding A&AEE at the time of Duncan's arrival, emphasised how crucial the establishment was to that process, while reflecting that budgets were still tight. Maund felt that, 'Unless other countries disarmed, we should have to re-arm to a position of equality, and if this came about, then he thought that quality in equipment would perhaps replace quantity, and that quality was, he felt, admirably maintained in our own aircraft industry by the co-operation which existed between the testing establishment which he commanded and the aircraft constructors themselves.'[xxv] This recognition would finally lead to an increase of new and more modern types arriving at the Suffolk aerodrome. Martlesham was to be busy over the next few years, and, under more scrutiny than ever, its stock continued to increase.

The phrase 'Martlesham is pleased' became something of a running joke in the aviation media, based on the frequency with which it was uttered by industry figures indicating the quality of a new aeroplane. The phrase was, according to *Flight*, 'About the highest praise which it is possible to give', on the basis that, 'By the time Martlesham has finished with a machine there are few of its features which escape scrutiny and comment. Consequently it is small wonder that if the officers and technical experts of the establishment are fairly unanimous in reporting favourably on an aircraft, that machine is as near perfect as doesn't matter.'[xxvi] Sir Richard Fairey, a giant of the British aircraft industry of the time who would later figure significantly in Duncan's career, was quoted as saying that, 'Martlesham was absolutely unique and that its value to the trade was very high, because it was the one place in the world where it was possible to have an aircraft tested and to get entirely unbiased criticism'.[xxvii]

In April 1933, Flight Lieutenant Menzies took up his post at the establishment. If his hope had been to fly a greater variety of aircraft types, he was not to be disappointed. In that first month his log book records flights in eight different types. And there was no waiting around – on the day of his transfer, Menzies was in the air in a Westland Wapiti K1129, exploring the handling of an aircraft that was new to him. (In fact, the Wapiti was only partially unfamiliar – the type shared the wings and tailplane of the DH.9A.)

A few days later, on 8 April, Duncan was trusted with an experimental type – although again this was a close relation of an aircraft he had considerable experience of. The Armstrong-Whitworth Aries J9037 was a prototype designed as an Atlas replacement, and was developed from that type, the major difference being the wings braced with zig-zagging 'Warren Truss' struts. Duncan flew this aircraft for an hour and a quarter, to an altitude of 8,000 ft, testing partial climbs. This term, deceptively simple-sounding, covers a series of tests to establish an aircraft's best rate of climb at various altitudes. It was exacting, repetitive, and required constant concentration. It was the perfect test to get a feel for the stuff a new test pilot was made of. Duncan flew the same aircraft again a few days later, testing climb and level speeds. Then it was the same task, but back with Wapiti K1129.

In truth, Menzies was still learning his trade as a test pilot rather than contributing to the test and development work. Both the aircraft were years old and would have been tested thoroughly already. But by the end of the month, Menzies had flown the Westland Wallace (a developed and stretched Wapiti) and a Hawker Hart light bomber, Hawker Demon (a fighter version of the Hart), Bristol Bulldog single-seat fighter, Armstrong Whitworth Atlas and Fairey Seal (a development of the IIIF powered by an air-cooled engine). By now Duncan was an experienced and skilled pilot who had been tested by endurance flights, serving at the margins of the Empire and instructing new pilots how to fly and fight. It's hard to imagine if he experienced any nerves or disquiet at the new tasks he was beginning to carry out; mild excitement and enthusiasm is perhaps more likely.

Test-flying, particularly today, has connotations of extreme excitement. Post-war films such as *The Right Stuff* and *The Sound Barrier* portray it as a romantic endeavour, an exploration of the unknown, the pilot and the engineer against nature. In the years before institutions began seeking records for their own sake, for publicity and to best rivals, test-flying was a sober business, both methodical and careful. The test pilot was not a buccaneering figure, nor was he liable to self-promotion. 'Loquacity is conspicuous by its absence from the demeanour of these gentlemen', was how *Flight* put it in 1935. Another report that year was more direct: 'If anyone intending to visit the Aeroplane and Armament Experimental Establishment, Martlesham Heath, on Empire Air Day (May 25) expects to be regaled with tales of how Martlesham pilots dice with death, cheat the grim reaper, and flirt with disaster, he will come away unsatisfied.'[xxviii]

Any aircraft arriving at Martlesham would have already undergone a programme of testing by the manufacturer to ensure that the aircraft was safe, basically sound in its structure and aerodynamics, and fit to be assessed by the service for which it was intended.

The prototype arriving at Martlesham would then undergo exhaustive tests of its performance, handling, maintenance, and, if a military aircraft, fighting qualities. These would begin on the ground, looking at seating position, access to the controls, view for taxiing and other assessments that could be carried out on the ground just as easily or more so than in the air. Weights, centre of gravity (C/G), engine vibration at different throttle settings, and readings from the cooling and oil system instrumentation would be checked.

At this point the aircraft – assuming no major faults had been identified in the previous assessments – would proceed to taxiing tests. These would address the suitability of the undercarriage – something Martlesham was well suited to test, as *Flight* described it as 'one of the worst-surfaced runways in the country'.[xxix] If an aircraft's undercarriage stood up to Martlesham's runway, it could handle any airfield. Wheel brakes and other features such as steerable tailwheel or skid would be thoroughly tried at this stage. The aircraft would be run at low speed and high speed, and its ground handling and the effects of the controls determined. This was of value not just in its own right but because a pilot could invariably tell a certain amount about the handling in flight of an aircraft from high-speed taxiing in relative safety. If any modifications were identified at this point, the machine would go straight back to the manufacturer.

When it was finally time to take the aircraft into the skies for the first time, generally at a light load, the pilot would typically allow it to run for some time on its wheels, after the tail had lifted, to test the controls. If all was well, he would lift the aeroplane off the ground and steadily climb. The approximate stalling speed would be established, but the aircraft not yet fully stalled. Apart from the basics, the pilot would be free to tackle the first flight as he saw fit. That might mean anything from a few circuits and a landing to aerobatics, depending on what he felt comfortable with and the machine capable of. Further flights would be made, exploring the performance envelope, handling in extremes, and at service load and overload, then different positions of the C/G to confirm the safe limits. True air speed would be measured by timing the aircraft along a straight stretch of local railway line at a particular altitude, after which the aircraft's Air Speed Indicator error could be calculated.

Often, 'short' handling and performance tests would be carried out to provide an initial report into the aircraft's characteristics, with the intention that later on a full, exhaustive series of tests would be carried out. 'Preliminary' or 'Short' performance trials might include partial climbs throughout the speed range, level speed and time to take-off, and the report might run to eight or nine pages. Often they were carried out with a specific purpose in mind, such as to explain loss of performance in older examples of a type against new ones.

A full test might run to fifty pages. An example from September 1936, for the Blackburn Shark, an aircraft Menzies was heavily involved with in testing, includes the following tests: performance at torpedo load; performance at reconnaissance load; consumption; oil suitability; cylinder temperature; handling; diving; spinning; weighing; flying qualities.[xxx]

Menzies' duties were similarly multifarious. The tasks he carried out on both service and experimental types recorded in his log books include level speed and climb tests, consumption tests, 'windmill' tests, handling with the C/G at different limits, wireless telegraphy and radio telephony tests, checking exhaust gas build-up, measuring oil cooling, cockpit heating, and assessing experimental equipment. The latter included a 'flight path recorder' (an early 'black box'), an experiment involving sound recordings of a Rolls-Royce Kestrel IIS engine in a Hawker Hart, and a 'Vibrograph' (vibration recording) test on a Vickers Vildebeest.

The first aircraft that appears with some frequency on Menzies' log books while at Martlesham is Westland Wallace K3562. This machine was no stranger to the A&AEE having first visited the establishment two years previously as the first production Wallace Mk I. This machine had been trialled at Martlesham in 1931 then returned to the manufacturers to upgrade to Mk II status before making its way back to the A&AEE for new-type trials in 1933. From 5–16 and 23–27 May, Duncan only flew this particular aircraft, carrying out handling tests with the C/G well aft of the established centre. This may sound straightforward, but the handling with the C/G so far aft could be difficult and uncomfortable, or dangerous even. Control inputs could have odd effects. Menzies undoubtedly approached this with his usual methodical and calm approach, but this was the first time he had been asked to fly an aeroplane near the margins of its safe configuration.

Accidents at Martlesham were rare but not unheard of. The careful, thorough manner of the A&AEE minimised them but could never eliminate the danger. Six months after Menzies joined the establishment, Flight Lieutenant G. L. G. Richmond was seriously injured when the prototype Boulton-Paul P.64 Mailplane crashed. It was seen to begin a flat turn that seemed odd to onlookers, before losing flying speed, then it stalled and fell. The reasons were never explained, and the conditions could not be assessed again because the Mailplane was completely wrecked. Richmond would recover, but it was a close call. Menzies was not flying that day – it was a Saturday – but was due to fly two days later. There is no question that he would have entertained any thought of not doing so, but that is not to say he had no misgivings. Such risks were part of the job.[8]

While the day-to-day flight testing of aircraft at the establishment was orderly to the point of mundanity, the A&AEE was a crucible of innovation and fusion of the newest thinking from other aviation sectors. There was no sense of superiority of military aircraft created to Air Ministry specifications – in fact, the Commanding Officer of the establishment would make it clear that the way military aircraft were created militated against the best performance, and the freedom enjoyed by designers of civilian aircraft allowed them to show the way. The establishment had a clear role in challenging orthodoxy.

At the time Menzies joined the A&AEE, the biplane was still the norm. Many new aircraft arriving at the Suffolk airfield still had substantial amounts of wooden structure, and most were skinned in fabric. Few aircraft could exceed 200 mph. During Menzies' two-year spell at the establishment, the winds of change began to blow through the industry with increasing strength. By the time he left in 1935, a handful of aircraft had passed through Martlesham that were of startling modernity. Particularly notable examples, in view of later developments in the field of aviation, came from Germany and the United States, or from commercial aviation and air racing, unshackled by the restraints of official specifications. Group Captain Maund strongly believed that civilian practice could lead military design. He pointed to the de Havilland DH.88 Comet's dominance in the recent MacRobertson Air Race, in the hands of none other than Tom Campbell Black, who had crossed paths with Duncan's squadron in Sudan more than once. Maund is reported to have,

> ... thought the very greatest credit was due to the de Havilland firm for producing the 'Comet,' which was a most efficient machine, as was shown by the fact that it attained a speed of 230 mph with engines totalling less than 500 hp. He thought there were three lessons which could be learned from the 'Comet.' It had definitely proved that high costs did not necessarily mean high running costs. The 'Comet' did eleven miles per gallon of fuel. There was a tendency in some quarters to regard high-wing-loading as very dangerous. He pointed out that during the race there were at least two forced landings by 'Comets,' both carried out without damage. The small structure weight of this machine indicated that high wing-loading was a good way of saving structure weight and getting a large disposable load.

With regard to typical RAF machines, Maund said he felt that, 'The "gadget king" had had his own way, and the performance was spoiled by projections and excrescences,' and that, 'On the whole he thought our aeroplanes were too large for the work they had to do.'

Maund was also keen to explore how greater co-operation across all parts of the industry could yield great advances: 'To get real improvement, what was wanted was teamwork like that which came into being in connection with the Schneider Trophy contests. The aircraft manufacturers, the engine firms, the research establishments and the pilots formed a team which produced wonderful results.' He suggested a similar approach to the next London–Melbourne race. Prophetically, he considered that military aircraft development should aim for speeds of 300 mph. Sir Richard Fairey, present at the December 1933 dinner, stated that he would like to see 'variable pitch airscrews, detractable [*sic*] undercarriages and some of the more modern forms of superefficient wings' developed.

This all serves to provide context for the situation in which Menzies began his long career as a test pilot. Moreover, it is a context of which he would have been acutely aware. While it might have been easy for the pilots of the establishment to have become buried in the detail of their work, too close to the wood to see the trees, Maund's leadership, and his insistence on involving the industry with the establishment's work, made it clear to pilots the overall purpose and scope of their activities. Moreover, Maund had the authority and initiative to drive that purpose. It was apparent that huge increases in performance would be realisable in the next few years through advances in aerodynamics, structures and engine performance.

The December 1933 dinner was probably the first time Duncan would have met Sir Richard Fairey, one of the figures helping to turn theoretical improvements into reality. It's easy to imagine that the great aviation pioneer and industrialist made a big impression with his vision of the future of aviation and sheer force of personality. And though most of the new military types appearing at the establishment at the time, and for the next few years, would be fabric-skinned biplanes, Martlesham knew what was on the horizon. Modernisation could not come soon enough. In 1934, *Flight* pointed out that a high number of types flying with home-based squadrons were obsolescent or would be within a year or two, including the Hawker Fury and Demon, Bristol Bulldog and Gloster Gauntlet fighters, e.g. the Hawker Hart, Fairey Gordon and Boulton-Paul Sidestrand bombers, and Westland Wapiti and Wallace general-purpose aeroplanes. They concluded 'before long, all the existing fourteen regular squadrons of fighters and three fighter squadrons of the Auxiliary Air Force will need re-equipment,' and 'in A.D.G.B.,[9] ten regular, two Cadre, and five A.A.F. squadrons of day bombers ... will all need new types either at once or in the not distant future'.[xxxi]

The establishment was preparing and helping the industry to take the next steps towards modernity as quickly as possible. But it would have come as a shock that the first such indication Menzies encountered was from a foreign aircraft industry – that of the old enemy, Germany.

At the end of the First World War, Germany had been an early adopter of new technologies: the self-supporting cantilever wing, metal frameworks, even duralumin skin. The restrictions of the Versailles Treaty had prevented the post-war development of these ideas in military aviation, but the German civilian aircraft industry had forged ahead (and would soon be doing so with increasing support from the Nazi government that had taken control in January 1933).

The Ernst Heinkel Aircraft Corporation of Warnemünde designed the He 64, a monoplane light aircraft, for the third International Touring Contest of 1932. It grabbed attention by pushing the top speeds seen in the contests up by some 40 km/h (from 200 km/h to 240 km/h) and completing the course of 4,700 miles in just three days – half the allotted time.[xxxii] The He 64 did not just display impressive performance though. It was comfortable, had excellent visibility all round and, most important of all, had a remarkably low stalling speed thanks to high-lift devices fitted to the leading and trailing edge. The 4:1 ratio of maximum to minimum speed seemed almost miraculous at the time. The National Advisory Committee for Aeronautics (NACA) described it as 'an achievement never before reached on an aircraft of this type,' adding, 'such a speed range is, indeed, exceled only by the Schneider Cup racers,' which, as indicated above, had been developed with significant input from the government, manufacturers, testing establishments, research facilities and engine builders. Three of the Heinkels had flown to Heston for a demonstration in September 1932 and caused even more of a stir.

The Air Ministry duly purchased an example and registered it G-ACBS for tests at Martlesham. Duncan first flew it on 1 August 1933, where he explored its handling, then again on 21 August. He was on leave during September, but on 6 October flew it again, testing climb and level speeds, and on 12 January 1934 for an engine test, which was repeated on 23 January.

If the Fairey Long-Range Monoplane had seemed a vision of the future of aviation, with its silver sleekness, size, solidity and huge span, one wonders what Menzies made of the He 64? Perhaps there was something in Maund's statement that British military aircraft were too big. The tiny Heinkel was a light touring aeroplane, of course, but it could carry two people in comfort at over 150 mph, with an endurance of 3 hours and a range of 559 miles. It did this on an engine of only 150 hp. And those high-lift devices on the wing allowed it to leap off the runway at an astonishing climb-out angle, even on the high wing-loading of 10.55 lb/sq. ft. It must have seemed that most commonly accepted ideas about aerodynamics were wrong, or at least had been interpreted far too

One of the aircraft Menzies tested at the Aeroplane and Armament Experimental Establishment, Martlesham Heath was the startlingly modern Heinkel He 64 touring aeroplane. (Author's collection)

conservatively. Nor was the He 64 constructed of expensive alloys, but of simple plywood. Its design touches were ingenious and practical – the wings, with their advanced features, were also neatly designed to fold for storage or road/rail transport and extend with no gap requiring a fairing strip. Both cockpits had full flying controls, but those in the rear cockpit could be locked off or removed (and replaced) straightforwardly. It was one thing to have an aircraft of exceptional performance like the Schneider Trophy racers or the Long Range Monoplane where all the design effort had gone toward a single outcome, but this was a practical aeroplane for everyday use with startling attention to detail.

Photographs of the aircraft demonstrating slow-speed flight show it hanging at a barely believable angle of attack, with the nose so high the wings of most aeroplanes would have long since stalled. The He 64 was recorded flying at 38.6 mph without losing altitude. If Menzies had come to Martlesham in the hope of flying machines at the cutting edge of design, experiencing extraordinary areas of flight, then surely he had found what he was looking for. The trials were of great interest generally, and formed the basis of a study for the Air Ministry's Directorate of Scientific Research.[xxxiii]

The He 64, however, was not perfect. Although the flaps and slots dramatically slowed the minimum speed, the maximum lift coefficient was 'reached at too high an incidence for a normal landing, and consequently much of the reduction in stalling speed has to be sacrificed'.[xxxiv] Even so, the landing distance was reduced by 24 per cent with the flaps and slots extended as much as possible to allow a reasonable landing angle.

The applications for military technology were not lost on anyone. The British aircraft industry seemed to be struggling to keep up with the advancements made by its German counterpart, despite the restrictions that had been placed on it. The Messerschmitt Bf 109 would be sooner to fly than the British monoplane fighters under development, and incorporated very similar automatic slots and flaps to the Heinkel, which the Hurricane and Spitfire lacked. It was also barely larger than the He 64.

But Martlesham did its best to keep the pace of change up. The Aeronautical Research Committee highlighted the A&AEE's findings during its studies into new low-wing monoplane aircraft such as the Heinkel He 64, showing the detail of the establishment's work:

> Reports received from the Aeroplane and Armament Experimental Establishment, Martlesham Heath, and elsewhere on the flying qualities of modern low-winged monoplanes have revealed interesting features. Directional stability is often remarkably good; some twin-engined machines can be flown on a nearly straight path on one engine without using the rudder, and with only slight yaw and sideslip. This result may be due to accident rather than to design, and is not altogether understood. Longitudinal stability is not always good. Conditions imposed on the designer may make it difficult to arrange the centre of gravity far enough forward; if so, the tail surfaces must be increased by an arbitrary amount, for there is little reliable information available to guide design. Accurate observations in flight are essential if progress is to be made rapidly, and we have recommended that routine tests of the longitudinal stability of all new machines should be resumed at Martlesham Heath as soon as possible.[xxxv]

This, among other things, made up Duncan's professional life.

But it was not all work at the A&AEE. Being back in the UK, with access to golf courses, Duncan took up the sport again with enthusiasm, playing for 'Martlesham and Felixstowe', presumably an association of the A&AEE and MAEE. On 14 April 1934, Duncan played against the Aero Golfing Society at Felixstowe Golf Club, losing to the Hon. Brian Lewis (the 2nd Baron Essendon, a racing driver who scored podium finishes at three Le Mans 24-hour races). Also playing were Sir Richard Fairey (for the Aero Golfing Society) and Flight Lieutenant Vivian Steel 'Lovely' Parker, who Duncan formed a strong friendship with.

There were other developments in Duncan's personal life. In 1934 or 1935, while on leave, he met Mary Margaret Scott Paterson, (who everyone, Duncan included, called 'Scott' or 'Scottie') at a tennis club in Tain, Ross-shire. There was clearly a strong attraction between the RAF officer and the daughter of a local farmer. It seems strange in retrospect that Menzies had travelled thousands of miles, to Egypt, Sudan, and Iraq, only to meet Scott a few miles from where he grew up. Within a year or two they would be married.

Over that time, there were an awful lot of aeroplanes to fly. A major development programme began, haltingly, in the summer of 1933 and progressed through the next two years, gathering pace towards one of the most significant aircraft in British history. The programme was for a naval multi-role aircraft that would be capable of less than half of Group Captain Maund's wished-for 300 mph and would have precious little of the modernity displayed by the Heinkel He 64. After the casual futurism of the Heinkel, the new naval 'Torpedo-Spotter-Reconnaissance' aircraft must have brought Menzies back to the present with a jolt.

Nevertheless, the aircraft Menzies helped to develop would enable the Fleet Air Arm to inflict major defeats on the Axis powers in the coming war, and do more than any other aircraft to save Britain from starvation. The great achievements of the Fairey Swordfish were not yet dreamed of, but they were breathed into life at Martlesham in 1934–35.

As a prelude, on 12 June Duncan flew a large biplane with the serial K3591. This machine was known simply as the Blackburn M.1/30A. It had originated, as the name suggested, from Specification M.1/30, issued three years before for a torpedo bomber, and incorporated some up-to-date features which were of interest to the Air Ministry, hence its presence at Martlesham. The new aircraft had an innovative fuselage, of completely watertight aluminium stressed-skin construction, and a 'wet' forward fuselage formed of stainless steel, which contained the fuel without any need for separate tanks. The wings featured full-span trailing edge 'flaperons' – control surfaces that had a dual function as high-lift devices to reduce the stalling speed. Much about the aircraft was new, and yet could it be said to represent the kind of advance over the preceding generation of aircraft that was needed?

Duncan flew the M.1/30A on 12 June 1933, then several times over 19–24 June – not as part of the trials but for the Hendon Air Display, to which the A&AEE traditionally brought a number of the new and experimental types on test that year. The redesigned aircraft by now almost met the performance required in the specification – its top speed was logged at 142 mph, and it could carry a military load of 2,735 lb. By now the Air Ministry had created a new requirement, but rather than focussing on improving performance, specification S.15/33 aimed to combine functions hitherto performed by separate types. The new type was to be known as the 'Torpedo-Spotter-Reconnaissance', or TSR. Three manufacturers, Blackburn, Gloster and Fairey, submitted designs, all of which were adaptations of existing aircraft.

Blackburn developed the M.1/30A into the B-6, powered by an air-cooled fourteen-cylinder Armstrong-Siddeley Tiger radial. The wings were improved with 'warren truss' struts, almost completely eliminating the need for external wires, and an innovative hydraulic locking mechanism while pneumatic wheel brakes were fitted. The B-6 joined the M.1/30A at Martlesham and Duncan flew both types in December 1933. It was not until June the following year that he got to compare the competing types, from Fairey and Gloster. This was in part because Fairey's initial submission, the TSR I (or TSR Mk I according to some sources[xxxvi]) had been destroyed in a crash during its contractor's trials when Fairey Chief Test Pilot Chris Staniland lost control. 'Chris did have a bit of trouble getting out of the prototype Swordfish during a spin', Duncan later recalled. 'He found himself back in the cockpit and had to get out again.'[xxxvii] The airflow literally sucked Staniland back into the aircraft. Eventually he was able to escape, but the episode emphasised, if any further emphasis were needed, the risks of testing new aircraft.

The design was reworked to eradicate the dangerous flaws and what emerged – the TSR II, registered K4190 – was now effectively the prototype of the illustrious Swordfish. It was unquestionably less innovative than the Blackburn. The main fuselage structure was a traditional steel-tube spaceframe, faired to a more aerodynamic form with light wood framing covered with doped fabric. There were no clever hydraulics, or trailing-edge flaps, although the ailerons could be drooped to provide a little of the same effect. It was powered by a 690 hp nine-cylinder Bristol Pegasus IIIM3.

In June 1934, Duncan was thoroughly pitched into the TSR development programme, repeatedly flying all three prospective types submitted to S.15/33. On 20 June, Duncan took off in the redesigned Fairey and subjected it to dives and spins. The design had been altered to try and alleviate the potentially deadly tendency to flat-spin that had briefly trapped Chris Staniland in the doomed aircraft, and would have been tested for its spinning qualities during manufacturer's trials. But even in 1933, spinning was not an exact science. As Staniland had found, an aircraft that had seemed stable and difficult to spin could, without any warning, exhibit a violent loss of control.

The aircraft had to be allowed to make at least eight revolutions before the pilot attempted to recover. It must have seemed an age, when there remained some doubts about the aircraft's stability. Fortunately, the TSR II displayed none of the alarming characteristics of its predecessor.

As if that weren't risk enough, dives had to be carried out too, and in the same flight, at various throttle settings. By 1933, the days of aircraft breaking up during their diving tests were relatively rare, though not unheard of. The terrifying-sounding 'terminal velocity' dive was the final such test, in which an aircraft was dived from not less than 20,000 ft until the aerodynamic drag prevented it from going any faster. This was carried out on all smaller aircraft – including light bombers, as by the mid-1930s they would be expected to reach their terminal velocity in ordinary use.

Menzies and K4190 came through the spins and dives unscathed. Then, six days later, he had to do it again, this time with an asymmetric load of three 250 lb bombs hung under the port wing. The handling of an aircraft with a 750 lb weight suspended a considerable distance off the centreline can be guessed at. It was probably not Duncan's most comfortable flight. Nevertheless, it was important to see if the Fairey could cope with such an unbalanced load, successfully pulling out of a dive without losing control or the loaded wing breaking off, in case an aircraft in service suffered a 'hang-up'.

The third submission was from the Gloster Aircraft Company. Gloster had originally developed an aircraft, the FS 36 (FS for Fleet Spotter), as a spotter-reconnaissance type for S.9/30. The company redesigned it with higher lift wing sections to allow it to carry greater loads and renamed it the TSR 38. It was conceptually similar to the other two aircraft, resembling the Fairey most closely. The chief difference was that it was powered by a Rolls-Royce Kestrel liquid/steam-cooled V-12 engine of 600 hp rather than an air-cooled radial. Duncan carried out handling trial flights on 13 June, then spins, climbs, dives, and various tests of equipment.

Reports from the A&AEE are overwhelmingly anonymous. Unlike RAE reports, which generally name the authors, the test pilots and other staff, who compiled the individual Martlesham reports are generally not known. This is partly because of the professionalism of the establishment – no individual was bigger than the whole – and also because the reports were so thorough many individuals will have contributed to the overall results. Duncan may have been the A&AEE pilot who remarked that the Gloster, 'Handled well between 90 and 115 m.p.h.' and that 'below this speed the control response was sluggish and manoeuvrability was poor.'[xxxviii] There is no way of knowing. In any case, he will have regarded his contribution as part of a collective effort.

A breakdown of Duncan's flights in the three TSR's in the second half of 1934 offers an idea of how involved he was in the programme:

3 August 1934 – flew prototype Fairey TSR.II from Fairey, Hayes, to Martlesham
14 August – consumption tests (Fairey and Gloster)
16 August – P.E. with Air Log (Fairey)
11 September – Climb and levels (Fairey)
12 September – Stalling speeds (Gloster)
17 September – Stalling speeds (Gloster)
18 September – Handling (Gloster)
21 September – Climb and levels (Blackburn)
27 September – R/T range (Fairey)
28 September – Dives (Gloster)
3 October – W/T (Fairey)
5 October – Rigging test (Blackburn)
23 October – Climb. Steam cooling burst (Gloster)
5 November – Air test (Shark K4295)
6 November – Climbs (Shark K4295)
8 November – Oil cooling climbs (Shark K4295)

At the time, the Blackburn B-6/Shark was somewhat farther along the course of its development and seemed the most promising of the three. Time would prove otherwise, though not until it had gone into service with the Fleet Air Arm. The Tiger engine was the Blackburn's Achilles heel, and it nearly proved Menzies' undoing as well, when picking up the prototype Blackburn after it had been returned to the manufacturer for modification to production standard. Even a delivery flight could be dangerous when it involved experimental or new aircraft. On 1 December 1934, Menzies flew Wapiti K1129 to Brough to collect the prototype Shark (now issued with the serial K4295) from Blackburns. The following is Duncan's record of the flight back:

I was flying down wind at 600 feet in bad visibility with a Wapiti in formation on the starboard side when the engine cut. An immediate gliding turn to port brought into view the only field that was green. It looked to be an impossible proposition but there was no choice.

I had to admit to myself that I was undershooting and damned myself for a fool, remembering the number of pupils I had told 'always take the far hedge when your speed has fallen off rather than undershoot and hit the near one.'

To my growing amazement it began to look as though I would make it. The Shark was on a light loading and cleared a six-foot hedge hitting the ground within 20 yards.

The aircraft had brakes but they were never used. The wheels sank in the soft ground of winter wheat which provided natural braking up to today's Maxaret standards and at the end of the run there was just sufficient room to walk between the airscrew and the far hedge.

The aircraft subsequently continued its journey by road and investigation proved that before this flight the fuel filter had been dropped. Although it was unknown at the time, this introduced an airlock into the flow from a tank designed to self feed into the main collector tank.

I take no credit for this approach and landing, it just happened. If I had had the extra height I prayed for I would have gone through the far hedge for a certainty.[xxxix]

Duncan's characteristic modesty aside, the landing was clearly a skilled piece of piloting, and he was commended for it by the officers in charge at Martlesham.

Testing of the TSR's continued into 1935. By the standards of the era, it was taking a long time to get the aircraft (first conceived in 1930) into service, even though the requirement called only for a relatively modest performance. The Shark entered squadron service later that year, and the Swordfish would follow a year later, when the aircraft were bordering on obsolescent. The year after that, the US and Japanese navies would introduce monoplane torpedo bombers that were between 50 and 80 mph faster.

Duncan had not just been testing the TSR's over this period. In fact, his whole A&AEE career is characterised by a variety of aircraft every week. While working on the naval aircraft, Duncan carried out a lot of flights on the Airspeed Envoy G-ACVI *Miss Wolseley* – a six-seat, twin-engined airliner with enclosed cockpit and retractable undercarriage. This particular machine had won the 1934 London to Johannesburg Air Race. It was faster in top speed and cruising speed than most of the military aircraft then at Martlesham.

Menzies also flew the American Vought V-66E Corsair K3561 (a biplane two-seat fighter-reconnaissance type), another of those aircraft that had been purchased for assessment. Why this machine was of particular interest to the Air Ministry is unclear – it was not of especially modern construction or impressive performance, although the

Menzies was ferrying Blackburn Shark prototype K4295 (rigged as a landplane) from Brough to Martlesham on 1 December 1934 when the engine cut and he had to force-land in a field. (It is seen here during floatplane trials at Felixstowe). (Author's collection)

Fleet Air Arm's increasing desire for two-seat patrol fighters may give some clue here. Duncan's most notable flights in the Corsair were four performances of aerobatics at the Empire Air Day display on 25 May 1935. The purpose of Empire Air Day was to open up service or experimental aerodromes to the public, to show their day-to-day work but also to make special demonstrations. At Martlesham, the public was promised 'Flying by experimental and service types,' as well as the usual workshops being open, some aircraft stripped down for observation, and a display of 'bombing up'.[xl] Duncan's penchant and skill for aerobatics, together with the unusual sight and sound of an aeroplane not seen anywhere else in the UK, must have made for a memorable display. It's easy to imagine Duncan's joy at being temporarily freed from the methodical shackles of partial climbs and oil cooling tests to throw an aeroplane around with something like carefree abandon.

For the most part, test-flying involved precious little of that. In the freezing winter of 1934–35, Menzies had been carrying out climb and level speed tests on Vickers Vildebeest Mk III K4164. It was a typically cold January day and there were forecasts of snow – probably one of the few occasions that flying for the sake of it was unappealing.

If the Fleet Air Arm's TSR aircraft were dated, the Vildebeest was verging on the fossilised. It might have been created specifically to demonstrate Group Captain Maund's lament about aircraft being 'spoiled by projections and excrescences' and 'too large for the work they had to do'. The Vildebeest, a land-based torpedo bomber, was vast for a single-engined aircraft, and a more inelegant contraption it would be hard to imagine. It was also extremely unpopular among the A&AEE test pilots. On the way back to

Vought V-66 Corsair K3561 was an individual example of the export model of the US Navy's two-seat fighter purchased by the Air Ministry for trials at Martlesham. Menzies demonstrated the aircraft to the public on Empire Air Day 1935. (Author's collection)

Martlesham after the morning's programme, the aircraft ran into a snowstorm. In 1961 Duncan wrote an account of what happened next, giving a fascinating glimpse into the uncomfortable realities of test-flying in that era:

> In the early 1930s crew comfort had little or no priority in the minds of those who wrote the Specifications. Some aircraft had a lever with 'Cockpit Heating On-Off' marked beside it but my memory of the Vickers Vildebeest is that it had no such lever at all. There was however a control which indicated Hot or Cold air to the carburettor.
>
> Of all the aircraft at the Establishment in those days the Vildebeest led the field in unpopularity when it came to finding a pilot to carry out a ceiling climb and full-throttle level in the winter months.
>
> Despite the pilot being placed so close to the Bristol Pegasus engine it was the coldest and draughtiest of the lot. At the finish of the test, height had to be lost in steps of 2,000 feet with a pause of some minutes while the pilot thawed out, tears streaming from the eyes and with agonising pains in all joints. There was no way of avoiding the pain, dress how one would.
>
> It was at the finish of the above flight that I found myself coming in from the North Sea over Felixstowe at 600 feet on course for Martlesham. A widespread snowstorm was coming down from the North and we were in the beginnings of it with visibility in the region of 2,000 yards. The snowflakes were increasing in size but I had had my flight and there was the usual coffee and warmth to look forward to in 'C' Flight office only 7 miles away. All seemed well.
>
> I knew the size and shape of the storm from studying it from above and I knew that if it got too thick for my liking I could turn out of it to the West and stand off for half an hour, by which time it would have cleared Martlesham. The aircraft was at full torpedo load with only 1 hour 15 minutes fuel used up so I had plenty of time in hand.
>
> We were down to 400 feet with 600 yards visibility deteriorating rapidly when I gave up all idea of coffee. The engine began to go rough and lose power; an instinctive forward movement of the throttle made things worse but a reduction in the setting put things right. The hot air intake to the carburettor was engaged and had been since the beginning of the let-down.
>
> Successive reductions in throttle setting in order to keep the engine running meant that we were not going to make Martlesham, not clear the storm, nor even stay in the air much longer. Trees, hedges and the occasional cottage were too close below our feet and I decided that the next hedge which came into view marked the down wind boundary of our field. With a loud bellow over my shoulder to Beale the throttle and switches were cut and we fell into a field the size of which was unknown.
>
> The Vildebeest had a tall hand brake lever on the starboard side of the cockpit operating an hydraulic master cylinder which gave differential braking by rudder bar movement. When the far hedge loomed up full port rudder produced a broadside slide and we ended up with the starboard mainplane three-quarters of the way across the Trimley St Martin–Martlesham Road without a scratch on the aircraft.
>
> A passing motorist gave me a lift to the Station Headquarters building where I reported to the Chief Engineer, McKenna, on the position of his aircraft and possibly expressed one or two opinions.

I must digress at this point to say that in the previous month I had made a forced landing at Fersfield in Norfolk when collecting the first production[10] Blackburn Shark from Brough.

Mac said he would come and look at the Vildebeest and we set off in his car. There was no conversation to begin with and then he said, 'Look Duncan, only last month you carried out the most exceptional forced landing and you appear to have got away with another one today. Don't make too good a story of it.' This remark didn't make sense to me but there was something about it which began to make me feel warm – but *not* to McKenna. I said, 'What the devil are you getting at Mac?' His reply was, 'You know quite well that you got caught out in this storm and had to land in a field. You tell the truth and I will see you all right but don't gild your story by bringing the engine into it.'

This was too much for me and I cannot remember the words of my reply. It was the 'I will see you all right' which really upset me so badly and I hadn't quite finished with him when we arrived at the aeroplane.

Mac started to look into the intake and I regret to say that I made a very audible remark to him in front of a number of onlookers to the effect that it was a curious type of engineer who would expect to find ice in a hunk of hot metal which had been standing in still air for half an hour.

Mac stopped looking for ice and an AA Scout, who had been directing traffic past the wing, came up to me and asked me if I was flying the aircraft. I gave him a not very encouraging affirmative whereupon he said, 'Good God, Sir, I thought you were on fire, clouds of black smoke coming out of you. I raced after you but took the Ipswich road.'

I looked at McKenna but said nothing. My attitude to the AA Scout changed completely.

Looking back on this incident McKenna was right. He had no cause to doubt my word and I don't think he did, but he was making quite sure that Vickers and Bristols were not put to unnecessary work in the way of a modification to the carburettor intake and that the Vildebeest programme was not delayed.

This brilliant landing once again won the plaudits of Menzies' superiors. The station commander at Martlesham wrote on the official report, 'I consider Flight Lieutenant Menzies did exceptionally well to bring the aircraft into forced landing without damage. This is the second effort within six weeks and the last was even more skilled.' The officer commanding the Performance Testing Section agreed, stating, 'It was an exceptionally fine show on the part of Menzies.'

Many of the machines Duncan tested were, like the Vildebeest, stultifyingly conventional. One of the most unusual, and the only rotary-wing aircraft Duncan would ever fly, was the Avro Rota K4320. This was the first of ten Avro 671 Rota aircraft ordered under contract No. 294074/33 for experimental trials. The Rota was a licence-built version of the Cierva C-30A autogiro. The RAF was considering the Rota for army co-operation use and the Fleet Air Arm for anti-submarine use, due to its short take-off and landing, and very slow flight capabilities. It was controlled like no other aircraft Duncan had flown, with a sort of 'tiller' altering the angle of the rotor blades to

In January 1935 Menzies made his second forced landing in six weeks when Vickers Vildebeest K4164 suffered engine failure in a snowstorm. The aircraft just missed running through a hedge onto the Trimley St Martin road. The snow on the propeller and the hedges can be seen clearly. (Menzies family collection)

effect changes in pitch and direction. He later recalled that it was easy to gain height but difficult to lose height. He is said to have claimed that to descend, he had to 'bounce it off a cloud'!

Later that year Menzies received a third rating of 'exceptional', a rare accolade. A further indication of the esteem in which he was held was soon to come.

A chance meeting back in July 1933 led to a dramatic change in Duncan Menzies' career a few years later. On that day, the 25th, Menzies flew an Armstrong Whitworth Atlas to Heath Row, Fairey Aviation's testing aerodrome, to pick up an aircraft. There he bumped into the company's chief test pilot, Chris Staniland – a well-known pilot through having been part of the RAF's High Speed Flight, and a racing driver of some note. Duncan took up the story in a letter of July 1976: 'I first met Chris in July 1933 when I went to Heath Row (as the RAF called it) but to Faireys was Great West. I was collecting a Gordon to take back to A&AEE Martlesham Heath. I met him on odd occasions until in 1935 he suggested that I got out of the RAF and join him at Fairey Aviation.'

Staniland and Menzies had become no more than casual acquaintances by the time of the former's suggestion. Nevertheless, Staniland was evidently sufficiently impressed with Menzies to recruit him. Martlesham test pilots were respected across the industry, and many had been recruited by aircraft manufacturers. Fairey may well have been aware of Menzies' work on the numerous examples of its own products that Duncan had evaluated during his test-flying career and with which 'Martlesham was pleased'. It's not clear exactly when the suggestion was made, but it evidently came out of the blue. Towards the end of July that year, it became a firm offer, with some urgency. On the 27th, Menzies wrote to the Commanding Officer of the A&AEE:

CONFIDENTIAL
A.&A.E.E.
Royal Air Force,
Martlesham Heath,
Woodbridge,
Suffolk
27 July 1935

Sir,
I have the honour to request that you will be good enough to forward this my application to resign my commission in the Royal Air Force.

I hold a medium service commission and have a total of two years service to complete, and while I realise that as state in para. 3535 of K.R. [King's Regulations] and A.C.I., medium service officers are only allowed to resign in very exceptional circumstances, yet I hope that in my case the circumstances will be looked on as exceptional.

My reasons for wishing to resign now are as follows:-

I have just been offered a post as test pilot to the Fairey Aviation Company. This offer has been made to me without application on my part, and is open for a fortnight only. This offer is to me literally the chance of a lifetime and will be missed if I am not allowed to leave the service at an early date.

Apart from my experience of test flying I have no qualifications whatsoever for civil employment, and it is very doubtful if I should be able to find a post at the conclusion of my commission in this branch of flying. I have always been interested in test work and the chance offered to me is one for which I am willing to make any sacrifice, and, although I can ill afford it, I am prepared to forfeit my gratuity if required to do so, provided I can take up this post as test pilot.

While I realise the fact that applications to resign from medium service officers will not be regarded favourably at this time of expansion, yet I venture to suggest that in the capacity of test pilot to a civil firm I shall be continuing to serve in a useful capacity to the Royal Air Force for many years, while if I complete my service in the normal manner I shall have to give up flying with the exception of reserve training, and my experience gained in the service as a test pilot will be wasted. Also having been at the A.&A.E.E. now for over two years it is probable that in the normal course of events I shall be posted to some other Unit shortly and the last years of my service will largely be spent in learning a new job.

The last thing I wish to do is to let the Service down in any way and I do trust that the Air Council will take the view that in my case the acceptance of a post as test pilot will enable me to continue serving the interests of the Royal Air Force for many years rather than leaving with no employment in two years' time.

I have the honour to be,

Sir,

Your Obedient Servant

The reason for the timing of the offer, and its brief window, may be connected with the death of Fairey test pilot Lieutenant S. H. G. Trower on 17 July. Trower had just completed a demonstration flight to the Belgian Air Force in the prototype Fairey Fantôme fighter at Evères when he crashed in the circuit to land and was killed. The company had lost an experienced test pilot at a critical time, when it was vying for contracts with several countries during a widespread period of air force modernisation and expansion. The opportunity to hire an experienced replacement, whose Martlesham career made him a known quantity, must have been a significant influence on Fairey's thinking. Sir Richard Fairey will have met Menzies through the Martlesham annual dinners and the golf matches with the Aero Golfing Society, as well as knowing of his work, and it is probable that his blessing was given to expedite the offer.

It was by no means a foregone conclusion that the Air Council would agree to release Menzies. While it was common practice to release pilots on Short Service Commissions – P. E. 'Gerry' Sayer (later the first Briton to fly a jet aircraft) had been allowed to cut short his own commission to join Hawkers in 1930[11] – Medium Service Commissions were quite another matter, and as Menzies pointed out, the RAF had embarked on a period of expansion and modernisation that meant experienced pilots were at a premium.

His arguments evidently persuaded 'Their Airships', however, for the Air Council agreed and on 24 August 1935 Menzies was transferred to the reserve of RAF officers. Two days later he joined Fairey Aviation as deputy chief test pilot.

Chapter 8

Fairey Aviation, Early Days, 1935–36

The work that the Fairey Aviation Company was then engaged in was tightly bound up with Martlesham's programme – the re-equipment, expansion and modernisation of Britain's military aviation.

At the leading edge of this movement were two monoplanes: the Battle light bomber and the Hendon heavy bomber. The company was strongly associated with naval and marine aircraft, with its background very much in floatplanes, but Sir Richard had never been satisfied to remain a niche manufacturer. With the Hendon and the Battle, Fairey was showing its ambition to be not just *a* major but *the* major supplier of bomber aircraft to the RAF.[12] Moreover, the company was now international, with a subsidiary in Belgium, supplying Firefly IIM fighters and Fox light bombers to that country's air force.

The Hendon dated back to a 1927 specification that was won by a more conventional biplane, but Fairey's audacity in putting forward a monoplane was rewarded, after further development, with production contracts. The Battle light bomber, by contrast, had beaten off competition from Hawker, Armstrong-Whitworth and Bristol to win Specification P.27/32 handsomely, and was ordered in quantity in June 1934 on the strength of the designs alone. In May 1935 this was confirmed and finalised, with Specification 23/35 representing a firm order for 155 aircraft (accompanied by the first production order of 200 Rolls-Royce Merlin engines). It was expected that more orders would follow, as indeed they did.

The company was in the process of significantly expanding its operations, particularly in the wake of the Battle order. Fairey purchased the old Crossley factory at Heaton Chapel near Manchester, and when this operation began in earnest Menzies would become the lead test pilot for aircraft produced at this site. His arrival was particularly timely for Fairey as the company would soon need an experienced test pilot to operate relatively independently of the Southern test-flying operation.

It would be some time before the production facilities were ready, however. Menzies therefore spent the first year of his employment at Fairey based at Hayes, flying mostly from Great West aerodrome. He was rapidly acquainted with Staniland's skills both as a pilot and a racing driver, the latter not always comfortably. 'He was a very able driver on a race track where the standard of discipline was high but I had many uncomfortable journeys with him on the high road, in his Bentley, where he made no allowance for fools', he wrote in 1976, adding, 'He was a superb demonstration pilot, his positioning and showmanship put him right out in front in those years.' From a demonstration pilot of considerable skill, this was rare praise.

There was little rest from test work between leaving one job and starting another. Menzies' last flight with the A&AEE was on 24 August (in Vickers Valentia K3603 as a passenger), the day of his release, and the previous flight on the 20th (piloting a Supermarine Southampton flying boat from Felixstowe). Interestingly, Duncan's last two flights while with the A&AEE were in large aircraft – a little preparation for the Hendon programme, perhaps? Duncan officially joined Fairey on Monday 26 August, and his first flight for the company was the following Wednesday, 3 September, in the company's de Havilland DH.60M Moth G-AARH, on an airscrew test. The following year, Fairey took out a patent for a propeller with a slot in the blade to prevent loss of efficiency in certain conditions, and it's likely that this is what Menzies was testing.[xli]

Appropriately, in view of Duncan's work on the TSR programme at Martlesham, much of his work after the first two months involved production and development test-flying for the Swordfish, checking handling, control and performance. The first Fleet Air Arm aircraft, K5660, rolled off the production line on 31 December, and Menzies flew it for a handling check on 6 January 1936. From the 21st, Menzies flew K5660 and its sister K5661 – effectively pre-production test aircraft – on a series of handling test flights, focussing on the ailerons. The prototype K4190, now back from Martlesham, also appears in Duncan's log books again. A great deal of this work involved the ailerons and lateral trim, which evidently at this stage was not perfect. Some tests were made with 'Flettner strip' (servo tab) adjusted, and others with the ailerons drooped a specific angle. In truth, the drooping ailerons of the Swordfish never had much of an effect, but improved feel at certain times. Lieutenant Commander Chris Götke AFC of the Royal Navy Historic Flight says of operating the Flight's preserved Swordfish: 'Just above where the pilot sits, there's a little wheel so you can droop the ailerons, so they're like flaperons. I'm not sure how many people use them, because what we find nowadays is that they make the ailerons very stiff, but they don't actually reduce the stall speed, but if you give it half a turn, it stops some of the snatchiness in the system. I usually put half a turn on [for landing].'[xlii]

Given the reputation of the Swordfish as an aircraft that was at the same time docile, easy to fly and highly manoeuvrable, the continuing work on the controls is illuminating. It illustrates the effort that went into making sure the aircraft behaved and responded as well as it possibly could in all circumstances. Fellow test pilot Captain Eric 'Winkle' Brown later praised 'the amiability and tractability of the Swordfish,' adding, 'I soon discovered that it possessed quite remarkable manoeuvring qualities which completely belied its appearance of unwieldiness. It could be stood on its wingtips and almost turned around in its own length!'[xliii]

There were also the inevitable spinning tests and adjustments to the elevators and fore-and-aft stability.

In each of these flights, Menzies would have gone through a number of evolutions as set down previously, perhaps testing modifications or adjustments, scribbling notes in response on the notepad strapped to his thigh. This item was common to test pilots everywhere – Duncan's was a flat aluminium case perhaps 6 inches by 4 inches, holding a small pad of paper where it could easily be written on, attached by a leather strap secured by a metal hook, which was much easier to remove quickly than a buckle. These notes would form the basis of detailed reports to the factory to enable alterations and improvements. The ability of a test pilot to accurately assess and communicate how the aircraft was behaving in flight in considerable, but salient, detail was crucial to their success. It's not unreasonable to suggest that Menzies' work at this stage of the Swordfish's career made a small but significant contribution to its legendary handling.

Towards the end of February, Menzies' work began to include the floatplane variant of the Swordfish. Fairey usually tested floatplanes from its facility at Hamble on Southampton Water. Several of these sessions over 5–6 March were recorded by a noted marine photographer, who captured some of Duncan's test flights. The images are as romantic as any that photographer took of the mighty pre-war racing yachts: the silver Swordfish skims across the broad stretch of glossy water, deltas of spray cutting back from the float steps, or bulls into waves, the propeller whipping the crests into spindrift. Four photographs found their way into Duncan's collection. Most of such flights would have passed without being immortalised in any other way than a few lines of text, but the sepia images capture something of the essence of pre-war test-flying.

Swordfish deliveries to the Fleet Air Arm were gathering pace at this time and Menzies was kept busy with acceptance flights before handover to the customer. March 1936 also marked two significant flights. That month was the first time Menzies came into close contact in the air with Battle light bomber prototype K4303. On the 18th he flew Swordfish K5932, with a Mr Rust as passenger, to take photographs of the prototype for the *Daily Mail*. The prototype had flown for the first time just a few days earlier, and the contrast between the sleek aluminium stressed-skin monoplane with its retractable undercarriage and enclosed canopy, and the Swordfish, with its fabric covering, cradle of

Menzies test flew prototype Fairey Swordfish K4190 at the A&AEE and with Fairey Aviation, including floatplane tests on Southampton Water in spring 1936. (Menzies family collection)

struts and wires, and open cockpits, would be hard to overstate – even though the biplane was only just going into service! Duncan would fly K4303 himself in April, demonstrating the new prototype to officers of the Belgian Air Force – several of whom he took up in it.

Duncan was undoubtedly busy at Hayes, but found time to marry Scott at Invergordon in April. The *Aberdeen Press and Journal* of 13 April 1936 covered the wedding as follows:

> Invergordon Bride
> Rogart Flight-Lieutenant as Bridegroom
> Much interest was taken in the district in the wedding in Invergordon Church of Scotland of Miss Mary Margaret Scott Paterson, Tomich Farm, Invergordon, to Flight-Lieutenant Duncan Menzies, son of Mr and Mrs James Menzies of Rogart, Sutherland.
>
> The Revs. Duncan Fraser, Invergordon, and D. MacCallum officiated.
>
> The bridesmaid was Miss Leslie Paterson, and the groomsman was Mr Jack Henderson, Dingwall.
>
> Over one hundred guests attended the reception, which was held at Tomich Farm.[xliv]

The following day's *Aberdeen Press and Journal* published a photograph of the couple taken just after the wedding on page 5 – the expression on Duncan's face is almost identical to the one he wore just before his first solo flight. Duncan had the week off, and was flying again by the following Wednesday. On his return, the testing of Swordfish resumed, though in June he took the opportunity to borrow Miles Falcon Six G-ADZL (a particularly rakish company 'hack') to take Scott, his new bride, flying from Great West to Martlesham and Hendon.

A Swordfish Menzies test flew extensively as a floatplane, K5662, the third pre-production aircraft, seen here in March 1936 testing handling characteristics with torpedo. (Menzies family collection)

Chapter 9

Stockport Heaton Chapel, 1936–38

After a long delay, by May 1936 the production of Hendon bombers was finally underway at Heaton Chapel, and Menzies was informed that in the autumn he would be required to start test-flying the aircraft. This would be from Barton, which served as Manchester's municipal airport until 1937, when the much larger site at Ringway was opened. 'I was given four months' notice by Major Barlow our General Manager at Stockport, and he said "I will need you on September 1st, 1936"', Menzies recalled during an interview with the Manchester Ringway archivist in 1988. 'Now four months is a very long time before that date. In fact I flew the first Hendon from Barton on 2nd September, one day after the estimated date put down for the first flight, which was rather interesting I thought. We flew fourteen Hendons from Barton. The Hendon was a large aircraft, over 100 ft. wingspan, and to get it into the main Hangar at Barton, it had to be put on skates and put in sideways.'

In September, Duncan took up his post at Fairey's Northern operation. On the 2nd, he made the first flight of a production Hendon, K5085, with the flight engineer Frederick Cale as his passenger. In a time where both society and the armed forces were still stratified according to class, Menzies was perhaps unusual in having a natural ability to win the loyalty of enlisted men and officers alike. One such relationship was with Cale, the flight test engineer who shared most of Duncan's flights in the production Hendons, and later many of his flights with Battles. According to Peter Menzies, Cale had great respect for Duncan, and named his son Colin Duncan in the test pilot's honour. Cale had worked for the Fairey Aviation company for many years before Duncan joined, having contributed to programmes including the Fox dual-control trainer and the Long Range Monoplane.

The Hendon took a long time to reach production, partly as a result of how advanced it was when it was conceived back in 1927, though Air Ministry vacillation also contributed. In fact, the Hendon's development spanned Duncan's entire RAF career! But Sir Richard Fairey's enthusiasm for forcing technology and its application were manifested in the huge bomber's cantilever monoplane layout. The design team that initiated the Hendon project had previously been responsible for the Long Range Monoplane, so they were in an excellent position to transfer the technology. The thick, high-lift Göttingen section wing and its internal structure with spar-booms braced against twisting loads by tubes arranged in pyramids was clearly derived from that of the Long Range Monoplane.

The Hendon had gone through extensive wind-tunnel model testing, developing details such as the wing section and undercarriage fairing shape, and the prototype first flew in

A Fairey Hendon visiting RAF Hornchurch runs up its two Rolls-Royce Kestrel engines. Menzies test flew most of the fourteen production aircraft and delivered several to the RAF. (Author's collection)

November 1930. After a crash in March 1931, the aircraft was rebuilt with substantial modifications resulting from the lessons of earlier test flights. Test flights continued throughout 1932, and when it became clear that the new generation of monoplane bombers – the Vickers Wellington and Armstrong Whitworth Whitley – would take longer than expected to bring into service, the Air Ministry ordered fourteen Hendons as an interim measure.

Even with such an extensive development period, the Hendon was not entirely right by the time the first production machines appeared in late 1936. Menzies was required to test the entire production run for lateral trim, and tail buffeting remained a problem. (He demonstrated the latter phenomenon to pilots of No. 38 (B) Squadron at Mildenhall on 22 January 1937.)

But the unrelenting and stressful business of production and test-flying had not dampened Menzies' enthusiasm for flying in the slightest. In November 1936, Duncan delivered the first RAF Hendon to an operational squadron, when he flew K5088 from Barton to Mildenhall in Suffolk. He wrote to his wife following delivery flight, describing 'a grand trip'.

Friday 20 November 1936
128 Piccadilly, W1
Dear Scott,
Just had a blether with you on the telephone and I hope you have taken your courage in both hands and decided to buy the dining room table, and the chairs and chest of

First production Hendon K5085 at No. 38 Squadron's Marham base, demonstrating its sheer size. Menzies delivered this machine to the squadron on 20 November 1936. (Author's collection)

drawers. I am very sorry for your sake, that you have got the responsibility of doing all this by yourself, but what of it? You are full of common sense and I have great faith in your judgement.

I had a grand trip today. There was miles and miles of fog but I was up above it in the most perfect weather and it was a fine day at this end. I had a lift down here this evening and Chris [Staniland] is coming in at 10.30 after some dinner or other and I am going down in the morning to fly one of the Hendons I took down earlier. I will be going back to Mildenhall on Monday morning and will I hope finish there on Tuesday.

My love to you both and don't be scared of finishing the house. Regards to Les,
Duncan

Menzies repeated the flight on 1 December and, using one of the dual-control Hendons, showed the ropes to the unit's commanding officer Squadron Leader S. M. Park and Flight Lieutenant Merton. The last few months of 1936 and first of 1937 were heavily occupied in production test-flying of Hendons from Barton, and occasionally delivering aircraft to No. 38 Squadron (the only RAF unit to operate the type).

Chapter 10

Battles and More Battles, 1937–39

In April 1937, the first production Battle light bomber, K7558, emerged from the Heaton Chapel factory, and while the last few Hendons were still to be tested, the new light bomber was now the centre of attention. On 14 April, at 16.10 in the afternoon, Duncan took the aircraft up for the first time.[13] This was the only machine he flew for the remainder of the month. The usual range of handling checks were carried out, though the overwhelming focus was on the Battle's level speed. These tests revealed the uncomfortable truth that production Battles, weighed down with additional equipment and built to mass-production standards, were slower than the prototype by around 20 mph – K4303's top speed (with an uprated Merlin F engine and variable-pitch propeller) was recorded as 257 mph, while the best K7558 could manage was only 238 mph.[xlv] Duncan flew the aircraft to Martlesham Heath for two days on 24 April, where the disappointing truth of the aircraft's speed was confirmed. Nevertheless, the Battle had been ordered in quantity and was vital to the RAF's modernisation programme.

The first production Fairey Battle, K7558, which had its initial flight by Menzies on 14 April 1937. (Author's collection)

After carrying out further test flights at Barton, Menzies flew it to Great West, as by then K7559 had joined the test programme (fitted with dual controls). After this, new aircraft came off the production lines at an increasing rate, while the prototype K4303 was now available at Barton too. A change in airscrew pitch was tried on 6–7 May, and level speed continued to preoccupy the test team. On 20 May, Menzies flew the second production machine to RAF Upwood, where he and Squadron Leader Parker, the officer commanding No. 63 Squadron, flew with dual control to acclimatise Parker to the type. This was repeated on 27 May, when Rolls-Royce test pilot Ronald W. Harker[14] was present, as part of efforts to maximise the Battle's performance or help the squadron with their operation of the new Merlin engine.

Meanwhile, the development of a more suitable flight test facility was underway. Fairey Aviation was instrumental in the development of Ringway, where Menzies was the first pilot to carry out a landing. This milestone was recorded in a typically understated manner in an interview with Manchester Ringway's archivist:

There was an occasion in December [1936] in which my General Manager at Stockport asked me, if my memory is correct, to take a Mr Hessey, who was understood to be a

The first prototype Fairey Battle, K4303, which Menzies flew a couple of weeks after its first flight. This could be him piloting the aircraft for photographer Charles E. Brown – the facial features, above average height and white flying helmet match, and he flew the aircraft numerous times in April 1937, when the photo shoot took place. (Author's collection)

member of the Corporation, over Ringway to see the site from above. There was no question of landing at Ringway on that date, as the grass strip about 300 yards wide, and 800–1,000 yards long, had been sown in September, and the ground was insufficiently firm, we would have gone axle deep had we attempted to land on that date.

Another flight which was of interest was coming up from Heathrow with another test pilot ['Freddie' Dixon] as passenger, and that flight was on the 17th May [1937]. The weather when we got to Congleton was very poor. Visibility was down to 500 yards and the nearest I was able to get to Barton was Sale, and I couldn't even see the canal. My passenger didn't like the weather conditions, and neither did I, and I returned to the grass strip which I had been watching for some months. As I lived in Wilmslow, I decided it was firm enough to land on, and we landed there as a matter of convenience – it was not an emergency landing, it was very suitable.[xlvi]

In June 1937, Fairey began to use the airfield at Ringway, even though the airport would not be formally opened for another year. Fairey staged its own opening 'on completion of their hangar for the final assembly of Fairey Battles'.[xlvii] On that occasion, Menzies was to have the honour of escorting Sir Kingsley Wood, Secretary of State for Air, and representatives of the government around the hangar, and then gave a demonstration of the Battle, described as 'spirited', in K7563, the fifth production example.[xlviii]

'On the 8th, the Fairey Aviation Co. gave a garden party opening of their small beginning', Menzies recalled of the 1937 event. 'At this garden party, a demonstration of the Battle was given, Alderman Toole, the Lord Mayor of Manchester, was the chief guest, Richard Fairey, Chairman & Managing Director of the Fairey Aviation Company was the host.'[xlix]

Menzies meets the Lord Mayor of Manchester after giving a display flight in a Fairey Battle K7563 on 8 June 1938 during the unofficial opening of Manchester Ringway Airport. Sir Richard Fairey looks on. (Menzies family collection)

In addition to the Battle, a demonstration of the Hendon and Swordfish was scheduled, as well as the 'Tipsy' light aircraft (named for its creator, E. O. Tips, General Manager of the new Belgian Fairey factory at Gosselies), operating from 'part of the landing area on the western side'.[1] This was followed by tea and refreshments in the marquee erected for the opening – though visitors from London had to leave promptly at 4.45 p.m. if they wished to catch the LMS 'Comet' from Manchester, to get them back to the capital by 9 p.m.

Also that month, June 1937, Menzies demonstrated Battle K7561 to the Belgian Air Ministry at Evere. Fairey had a close connection with Belgian aviation, having set up the *Societé Anonyme Belge Avions Fairey* subsidiary in 1931, and was hoping to sell Battles to the Belgian Air Force. The demonstration was a success and Belgium ordered sixteen Battles, which were to be built by Fairey at Stockport (not Gosselies, as is sometimes stated). These machines had slight modifications to the RAF standard, including a longer radiator intake fairing, and were reputedly slightly faster than British equivalents. With Battle production, and consequently test-flying, ramping up, Menzies gained an assistant test pilot to help with the burden in October 1937. Flight Lieutenant Sam Moseley was to become a key part of Fairey's northern test-flying operation, especially with war ever more likely.

A few days after the demonstration in Belgium, Menzies had the first taste of the aircraft with which he would later be associated more than any other – the Fulmar. Fairey had developed the P.4/34 light bomber in response to an Air Ministry specification, and although it was rejected in that role,[15] the design was resurrected by Fairey and offered to the Admiralty as an interim naval fighter. The idea of a light bomber being converted into a fighter may seem illogical, but two-seat long-range fighters were central to Fleet Air Arm doctrine in the late 1930s due to the perceived need to carry a navigator. Meanwhile, the two-seat fighters the Fleet Air Arm currently operated were beginning to look horribly inadequate. The Blackburn Skua was supposed to combine the roles of dive-bomber and fighter, with the emphasis on the former. It was an effective dive-bomber and proved reasonably good at tackling bombers, but was largely helpless against single-seat fighters. The Roc was an adaptation of the Skua with a four-gun powered turret, in the style of the RAF's Boulton-Paul Defiant. Some voices in the Air Ministry called for the two aircraft to be cancelled before they even went into service, so unsatisfactory were they as fighters, but there was nothing to replace them with. Fairey, however, realised that it had in the P.4/34 an aircraft that could comfortably outperform the Skua and Roc, offered comparable range and load-carrying ability, and had already amassed significant flying time in prototype form. The company offered an interim fighter based on the light bomber around January 1938. Menzies flew the second prototype P.4/34, K7555, at Great West on 27 June, carrying out handling trials as part of the preparations for the Fulmar programme.

There were happy matters at home too. Duncan became a father in 1937 with the birth of his daughter, Mary Ann.

The official opening of Ringway, a year after Fairey's private opening, was a rather more spectacular affair, befitting Ringway's status as a true regional airport. Three airlines – the Dutch service KLM, the Isle of Man Air Service, and the Railway Air Services – operated there from the launch. But the opening was a martial affair too.

The Sudeten crisis was unfolding in Europe and war was looking increasingly inevitable. Though no military air units would be based at Ringway for the time being, the opening event was dominated by squadrons of RAF aircraft, demonstrations of aircrew training and air drill with Gladiators, Battles and Harts of local squadrons. Most ominously, an anti-aircraft battery was available for the public to look around. It was reassuring to know that there were defences against air raids, but it brought home the likelihood that those raids would take place.

Fairey had two hangars at Ringway now, the second having been moved from Barton and put to use as the paint shop. The only area of tarmac on the whole airport was in front of these buildings – at the time, the landing area was entirely grass. Further hangars would be added in time, and by the end of the Second World War there would be six hangars relating solely to Fairey's operations there.

For Duncan, the vast majority of the period from 1937 to 1939 was taken up with production testing of Battles, which were then pouring off the Heaton Chapel production line. It cannot have been suspected just what a waste of production effort the Battle represented. The best that can be said is that the programme prepared many RAF bomber squadrons for modern machinery and the industry for producing it – and many of the aircraft produced did at least find vital employment in second-line roles, as training aircraft, target tugs and testbeds. The Battle was far from the only type entering service in the late 1930s of which much was expected but turned out to be flawed in its intended role, but this was still some time away. In September 1938, another factory began turning out the type. On 21 July 1938, Menzies flew Battle K7587 to Ringway from Longbridge where Austin Motors had been using the machine as a pattern aircraft. The first Austin-built Battle, L4935, flew the next day and Duncan was present, although he did not take the machine up. He did, however, fly it extensively at Ringway from 9 September as part of the flight trials of the Austin-built aircraft.

By the end of 1938, over 400 machines from the RAF contract, plus the sixteen Belgian Battles, had passed through the Heaton Chapel test pilots' hands.

At the outbreak of war in September 1939, around 800 Battles had been delivered to Air Ministry contracts. Advances in aviation had been so swift, however, that what had been the most modern light bomber in the world a few short years before was now obsolete, at least in the circumstances in which it had been required to operate, without local air superiority or much in the way of fighter escort. Ending production of the type was out of the question, as there was nothing ready to follow it at Heaton Chapel, so Battles continued to be built simply to keep the production line open. An increasing number of the machines tested by Menzies and his assistants were built as trainers and target tugs, and many Battles returned to Heaton Chapel to be reconditioned and converted to second-line duties.

In May 1939, Duncan had visited his old workplace of Martlesham Heath and flew the first production Hawker Hurricane Mk I (L1547) and Spitfire Mk I K9793. War clouds were on the horizon. Was Duncan taking the opportunity to take a peek at the machines he might be called upon to defend his country in? A year later he would write to Scott, suggesting that he would have no objection to being called up if he would get to 'go after them' in a Hurricane or Spitfire.

Life went on. Duncan's second child, and first son, Sandy, was born in 1939.

Early production Battle K7572, which Menzies first flew on 15 August 1937 from Fairey's new test flying base of Ringway, is seen here with a Miles Falcon Six. (Author's collection)

As war approached – inexorable, unstoppable – preparations began at Heaton Chapel for the Battle's successor on the production line. This would be for another machine that was arguably underpowered, too slow and overloaded, but which would by no means be the waste of resources the Battle was. The Fairey Fulmar would indeed see the Fleet Air Arm through its toughest challenge and, together with a handful of Martlets and Sea Hurricanes, and of course Swordfish, help the Royal Navy gain the ascendancy in the Mediterranean.

The Admiralty agreed to an order of 127 fighters based on the P.4/34 in March that year, despite misgivings, and the Air Ministry agreed on the basis that the Roc still looked likely to fail completely (though in the event, 136 were built and the type did briefly see frontline service). On 5 May 1938 a production order for 127 aircraft, of the type proposed, was offered to Fairey, to be named Fulmar, after a type of gull. No prototypes were required, as the P.4/34s could serve that role, and the first aircraft to contract, 752200/38, would be the first of the serial block N1854–N2016. Fairey began tooling up for production and, in the meantime, construction of the first two Fulmars, which were essentially hand-built. They would be constructed as closely as possible to production standards but were to all intents and purposes pre-production machines with which to carry out trials.

Menzies flew the P.4/34 prototype K7555 at Great West on 14 June 1939, taking part in stall-handling tests after the aircraft had had its wings and tail modified to better replicate the handling of the Fulmar. Indeed, the aircraft was later recorded in Duncan's log book as the 'P.4/34 Fulmar'. The Admiralty's Naval Air Department (NAD) was concerned to ensure the safe behaviour of the aircraft at the stall and requested either wing slots or an anti-spin parachute. The P.4/34 had not exhibited problematic stall characteristics but the A&AEE tests had reported that it was 'easy to stall' if attempted deliberately. The Blackburn Skua was known to have a vicious and incurable stall, and may well have been on NAD's mind when this requirement was made. Fairey was concerned at the additional weight this would add but promised to investigate further.

With 8 inches removed from each wing and the tailplane position changed, Chris Staniland flew the altered machine at the Great West Aerodrome. He reported: 'As far as can be seen this made no difference at all, the machine at this load behaving very well at and around the stall. It has no vicious tendencies and in fact has to be held up definitely if it is required to stall the machine.'

When the aircraft was tested at a greater weight the response was found to be the same – if the controls were released or centralised at any time, the aircraft would immediately recover from any incipient stall. In other words, the aircraft's stalling characteristics were very good, and, if anything, better than they had been.

This established satisfactorily, Menzies flew K7555 to Ringway on 3 August, presumably to help the factory at Heaton Chapel prepare for production and perhaps to give the test pilots some experience, and returned it to Great West six days later. A month after that the German military invaded Poland, and Britain and France declared war on Germany in response. This was a situation for which Duncan, the company he worked for and the air arms they supplied, had been preparing for. Now the strength of those preparations would be tested.

Chapter 11

War and the Fulmar, 1939–42

As far as Duncan's log books are concerned, initially it seems the outbreak of war had not affected his work. He continued production testing Battle after Battle. The prototype Battle Trainer, P2277, appeared in October 1939, already indicating that the type's purpose was beginning to move away from frontline roles. The Battle Trainer had a significantly different appearance to the bomber version, with two separate fighter-style cockpit enclosures rather than the more familiar single long canopy. Handling trials with Frederick Cale as flight test engineer began on the 27th.

At the beginning of November, Duncan notes in his log book the initial flight of the 859th Fairey-built machine for the UK Air Ministry. On the 30th, full dual controls had been fitted to P2277 and Duncan flew the aircraft from the rear cockpit. In December, Menzies demonstrated the prototype for Training Command HQ.

The Fairey Fulmar was about to become Duncan's main focus, with the Battle still in production but its development complete. Like many Fleet Air Arm types during the Second World War, the Fulmar was an aircraft of contradictions. It was generally popular with its crews, who nevertheless regretted its mediocre performance. It was the mainstay of the Fleet Air Arm's fighter squadrons for a relatively short period during the Second World War, between 1940 and 1942, yet it was the most successful fighter in Royal Navy service, with 112 kills.

In January 1940 the first aircraft, N1854, was completed, some three months after the first delivery was supposed to have been made to the Fleet Air Arm. Duncan took it up for its first flight at 3.10 p.m. on 4 January.

N1854 would go on to experience a varied and lengthy career – indeed, it was still flying twenty years after the Fleet Air Arm had replaced the last frontline Fulmar in the day fighter role, and nearly a decade after the last aircraft in RN service was scrapped. In that time it was flown by some pilots of considerable distinction and carried passengers of equal note. But the story of N1854 is, more than anything else, Duncan's story – the story of a man and his aeroplane.

For now, it was the story of readying a much needed machine for service, and attending to the details. 'On the first flight we had rudder instability, and this was cured by an increase in mass balance on the rudder, forward of the hinge point,' Menzies recalled in his interview with the Manchester Ringway archivist, Brian Robinson, in June 1988. By 16 January 1940 the new rudder had been fitted and flown. This was not the last that would be heard of rudder instability, however.

The first Fairey Fulmar, N1854, the aircraft Menzies would be associated with more than any other. It served as prototype, testbed and then communications aircraft for Fairey Aviation. (Author's collection)

Menzies' log books reveal frustratingly little about those early flights, but in itself this suggests there was little to report. The modified rudder was fitted in time for N1854's fifth flight, on 16 January, and Menzies continued testing the new fighter without incident. The first flights were all relatively short, between 10 and 45 minutes, and were spent exploring the Fulmar's performance and handling.

The final inspection conference took place on 7 March, when the Admiralty studied N1854 and requested a number of small modifications to production aircraft relative to the first aircraft's cockpit layout, gun installation and ground equipment, and also asked for armour protection covering a 15 degree angle off the fore-and-aft axis.

For the first three months of 1940, N1854 was the only Fulmar in existence, only being joined by N1855 in early April. When the second Fulmar became available, more specific testing could begin. With N1854 acting as the 'baseline' aircraft against which alterations could be compared, N1855 was used to explore different aspects of the aircraft's design and construction, for example 'chassis [undercarriage], elevator, rudder' and 'reversal of lateral trim', while a 'special airscrew' and revised ailerons were trialled. Meanwhile, N1854 continued its general test flights, remaining in the same specification it had been since the modified rudder was fitted.

The war had not yet penetrated into every area of life, as a letter Menzies received from a friend at the end of April attested. There was at least some good news, it seemed. Rupert Hartley Watson had served in the RAF with Duncan, and had remained in the service, joining No. 504 (City of Nottingham) Squadron in 1936:

The Officers Mess
RAF Debden
Saffron Walden
Essex
28/4/40

Dear Duncan,
I hope this will find you.
We are stationed here at Debden but go to Martlesham every other week for a week at a time. Going there again on Tuesday. We ... do day and night duty and chase anything that comes along. Damn few come our way though. We got a Heinkel about a month ago but have seen nothing since.

I beat James to it after all as far as promotion goes. I got mine in January. I have been commanding the squadron since then. James also is a Sq/Lr but in the operations room at the moment. He had a bad crash at the start of the war and got spinal concussion. He's just about fit to fly again now.

I'm getting married up in Town on June 1st it's a Saturday and I wondered if there was any chance of you doing best man for me. I should be very pleased if you would and you won't be overworked or have to do anything uncomfortable like making a speech. The invites are not out yet but I'll send you and Scott our dates. How is she? Will you send her my kind regards.
Sorry this is rather short notice.
All the best
Yours
Hartley
PS if you've been promoted please excuse the wrong rank

Duncan wrote straight back. The reply he received was not, however, from Hartley Watson:

Dear Mr Menzies,
I write without being sure if I have your name quite right or if you have some rank of which I do not know as Rupert always spoke of you as 'Duncan'. A letter of yours to him was forwarded here from Debden. We opened it but have only read the concluding remark just above your signature: 'Best of luck and don't go too quickly.' So you evidently knew him well and realised that he might be too eager. I have no idea if you had any mutual friends and have heard from them what happened but in case not I am sending a few particulars herewith. You will know the sort of son we have lost and how bitter it is – our other boy four years ago.

If ever you can come to see us my husband and I will be delighted; Rupert always spoke of you as a real friend and I am such a proud mother that I know you must have been fond of him.
Yours sincerely,
Iona Hartley Watson

Squadron Leader Rupert Hartley Watson had taken off in Hurricane L1947 on a night patrol on 30 April, just two days after he had written to Duncan. When returning to Martlesham Heath the Hurricane crashed at Ditchingham, around 30 miles north of the airfield. Hartley Watson was killed. Duncan kept both letters all his life. It clearly affected him deeply. Scott wrote on the envelope, 'Letters from Hartley (another dear friend) – and his mother, poor lady – he was such a fine fellow, and so full of fun.' Duncan would lose many friends throughout the course of the war, but Hartley Watson was the first, and the loss, with the circumstances, must have been devastating. Peter, his youngest son, recalled his father telling him that he felt that 'if he hadn't gone to Fairey Aviation he would not have survived, as so few of his contemporaries made it through the war'. Considering the dangers of test-flying, and the roughly one in four chance of test pilots dying, this is a sobering thought.

But, as ever, there was work to do, and Duncan had to get on with things. On 2 May, he tested revised ailerons on Fulmar N1855, after which it was cleared for delivery to the A&AEE – which had moved to Boscombe Down in Somerset, further away from German bomber bases – and Menzies took the Fulmar there on 3 May. Once again, N1854 was the only Fulmar at Ringway available for manufacturers' testing, although it would not stay there long. Within weeks, as soon as there was another Fulmar to carry on manufacturer's testing, N1854 would join N1855 at the A&AEE. Menzies wrote to his wife on 23 May referring to a trip in which Sam Moseley delivered a Fulmar and Duncan accompanied him in the Stinson communications aircraft. It was probably N1854 that Moseley delivered – N1858 soon followed, after no more than a couple of flights at Ringway. Menzies himself took part in some of the A&AEE trials, including spinning, with weight at the forward C/G limit and 10 per cent aft of the aft limit.

Menzies flying early production Fulmar N1858 in 1940. (Author's/Menzies family collection)

That month, Duncan relocated his young family to Scotland, as far from the war as he could get them. The letter to Scott shows that there was more on Duncan's mind than test-flying. It swings between the domestic (he mentions the travails of the gardener), the professional and the dark shadow of the war. France was overrun and Duncan thought there was every chance he would be called up to fight at any time. This did not seem to cause him any great distress. He had, of course, served in the RAF before; those he had served with, like Edwardes-Jones, were in the thick of it, and Hartley Watson had already given his life, though Menzies still did not know the circumstances. As an anonymous 'Airman's Letter To His Mother',[16] shortly to become famous, put it, 'No man can do more, and no one calling himself a man could do less.'

23 May 1940
Dear Scottie,
I think I wrote to you last on Thursday evening and posted it in Wilmslow on Friday morning when I called at the house to see Jones. He was in very good form but people have been stealing plants and he is very annoyed. He tells me he has joined the anti-parachute brigade but how much truth there is in that I don't know.

In the afternoon Sam took a Fulmar to Boscombe and I went down in the Stinson calling on Jerry [Sayer, Gloster test pilot] at Brockworth for a parachute I left there the last time I was South. Sam and I went on from Boscombe to Gt West in the evening and spent the night in London. London is very dull. I spent the night at the club and Sam with his mother. We went back the following morning by train and I spent the day at Hayes. I spent last night with Chris [Staniland] who is just the same as ever. After supper we went out for a glass of beer. I got back to Ringway in time for lunch at the works this morning. We saw Churchill returning from France yesterday afternoon escorted by 8 Spitfires. They passed over the aerodrome just before we left.

I found letters no. I and II at Ringway for which many thanks. I haven't heard yet what happened to Hartley but I will one of these days. I told his mother that both you and I would visit them if we were in the neighbourhood.

All of our people got away from Gosselies in Belgium alright and are scattered about France at the moment.

Tillyer who is one of them sent his wife and child to England last September and like a fool came over 3 weeks ago and took them back to Belgium.

Greece is off and so alas is my cruise with the Fulmar. It is a pity but it can't be helped. [Foster H. 'Dicky'] Dixon was told yesterday that test pilots might be called up any time. Having got you and the children parked now I don't think I would grumble much, especially if they gave me a Spitfire or Hurricane to go after them in.

Very good you have got Nannie back to give you a hand. It must be a job coping with Sandy and Jess. You stick at both of them. Goodnight Scottie old thing.
Love Duncan

Duncan had caught sight of the Prime Minister's aircraft, the No. 24 Squadron de Havilland Flamingo R2764, escorted by eight Spitfires of No. 92 Squadron,[17] as it returned from Le Bourget to Hendon. Churchill was engaging in urgent shuttle diplomacy with the French government in a desperate attempt to shore up resistance to the German advance. Just an hour after returning, Churchill would meet with the War Cabinet. While Duncan cannot have known the precise purpose of Churchill's presence that day, it must have been clear that the war was not going well for the Allies. Belgium had all but fallen, and Menzies was naturally concerned about the staff at Avions Fairey. The factory had been heavily bombed on 10 May, the day of the invasion, just as the first Hurricanes were nearing completion. The General Manager, E. O. Tips, managed to evacuate the personnel and some equipment to France, where preparations were made to take a ship from Saint-Nazaire for England, but the ship was sunk by an air raid just after leaving harbour. Fortunately, most of the staff survived and many went on to work for Fairey in the UK.

One of those who escaped and joined the parent company was Albert Eyskens, test pilot with Avions Fairey, who was seconded to the RAF on reaching England but was then released to join Menzies as his second assistant. This was just as well, and not just for Eyskens, as the work of the Fairey 'Northern' operation was ever-increasing. As well as Fulmar development and the testing of reconditioned Battles, Fairey had taken on the management of the Burtonwood repair depot, and occasional test flights were required on repaired and reassembled American aircraft (examples being a Northrop A-17A Nomad and a Curtiss SBC4 Cleveland on 5 August 1940). In the event, test pilots were not required for front-line service, which was ultimately fortunate for the war effort – test-flying was risky enough and carried a certain attrition, but the loss of experienced development pilots to frontline squadrons would surely have seriously hurt Britain's attempts to develop new aircraft as the war progressed. The purpose of Menzies' cancelled visit to Greece is unknown, but the country had bought Battles and was possibly interested in other Fairey types. A sales tour in the Fulmar was also, unsurprisingly, called off. The extent to which Britain's back was to the wall is evident even through Duncan's breezy tone.

Duncan was keeping in touch with his RAF comrades, not least those in frontline squadrons. In June 1940, on the way back from a flight to Great West, he paid a visit to E. J. (Humphrey Edwardes-Jones), who had been promoted to Wing Commander just a day or two previously. E. J. was then in command of No. 17 Squadron. The Battle of France was reaching a climax, and though the stakes were as high as at any point during the war, Duncan's letter to Scott shows distinct *sang froid*. Whether this was how Duncan felt, or putting a brave face on it, he showed great confidence in the RAF fighter pilots:

I landed at Wittering on the way back and had an hour with E. J. His Squadron had just had 6 days of Dunkirk and were in terrific form. I heard a lot of Blood and Thunder which might not appeal to you but interested me enormously. They got 16 confirmed and 14 unconfirmed. He claimed it was difficult to get confirmation as there was such a shemozzle. They lost 10 machines but only four pilots as the other 6 were fished out of the channel. Jones says it is grand fun once you get cracking.

They have all got their tails right up in the fighter squadrons. E. J. has Hurricanes.

I got back here at 8.30 pm last night and it was lovely coming over the river ... I wished you had been with me.

I have been to Wittering this evening at 5.30 and go again next Wednesday at the same time so you will know where I am if you are not too busy.

The core of the test-flying team at Fairey's northern operation in 1944. From left to right are Sam Moseley, Duncan Menzies and Albert Eyskens. Note Menzies' notepad with thigh strap for making notes while carrying out test flights. (Menzies family collection)

Menzies notepad holder with strap, similar to the one he is seen holding in the previous photograph. (© Matthew Willis)

I have found a flat about 10 mins from here and sat in the lawn on the bowling green ... Absolutely fine. No one but myself, my pipe and a pint of beer.

Unlike the vast majority of Duncan's RAF friends and acquaintances, E. J. would survive the war, eventually rising to the rank of Air Marshal.

Meanwhile, A&AEE trials of N1854 and the other two Fulmars proceeded satisfactorily, with no major problems encountered. A report from November 1940 indicated that 'The aeroplane is easy and pleasant to fly,' also noting it was 'easily manoeuvrable at its top speed.' However, the report went on to say that the Fulmar, 'Cannot be said to be very manoeuvrable in comparison with a Hurricane, mainly because of the heaviness of its ailerons in the dive ... In comparison with present day fighters the Fulmar has a low top speed. The rate of climb and ceiling are both low for a fighter.'[li]

The trials with N1854 and its sisters by both Fairey and the A&AEE had uncovered some uncomfortable facts. While the Fulmar had fine handling qualities, it had met none of the Admiralty's performance requirements, even those which had been relaxed to expedite rapid production. The reasons for the performance shortfall can at least partly be attributed to the Admiralty's equipment and other requirements, such as the taller cockpit canopy and increased tail incidence, but whatever the reason, the Fulmar Mk I was some 20 mph slower than required (40 mph slower than the less powerful P.4/34) and was over 1,000 lb heavier.

New production Fulmars were coming off the Fairey production line every few days while N1854 was at the A&AEE, and these helped replace the first machines in the manufacturer's testing programme. The pace of testing was high because it was imperative to get the aircraft into service. It was already late, and the shortcomings of the Skua and especially the Roc had been starkly highlighted during the recent Norwegian Campaign.

The internal Fairey newspaper, *Fairey Affairs*, stated in 1958 that, 'The speed with which this aircraft was introduced into Squadron service was so remarkable that it is worth recording.'[lii] By the end of April, the first 'proper' production Fulmar, N1856, first flew (Menzies refers to it as '1st production' in his log book, and Fairey Affairs called it the 'first of the Production Trials machines'). In just over six weeks, the first three full production Fulmars were delivered to No. 806 Naval Air Squadron to begin to convert from its Skuas. That this was achieved is a testament to what Captain Eric 'Winkle' Brown called the 'basic rightness' of the Fulmar, but it is also a testament to the early work carried out in N1854. Brown described the Fulmar as, 'A forgiving aeroplane and even the most ham-fisted of pilots could usually put it on the deck without bending anything.'[liii] Soon, 806 and 807 Naval Air Squadrons received Fulmars and were operating from carriers in the Mediterranean during the most hard-fought phase of the war for the Royal Navy.

When N1854 returned to Stockport from the A&AEE, its status as the aircraft against which all others were measured had passed. It was now just another Fulmar during a period of heavy testing for production improvements and modifications. Throughout September and October 1940, Menzies flew the first Fulmar for tests of a new high-speed hydraulic accumulator system (which permitted the faster deployment of undercarriage and flaps, and wing folding).

Towards the end of 1940, steps were being taken in the Fulmar programme to improve performance. Fairey had from the beginning pushed for a more powerful engine. The number of Fulmars on order had been raised from 127 to 250, and it was decided that machines from the 150th onward would be powered by the Merlin XXX (30) when this became available (in the event, the change was made at the 154th aircraft). The Merlin XXX offered a significant increase in power over the existing Merlin VIII, and various detail changes that had been in the pipeline were included as a package, and the aircraft gained a new designation in the process – Fulmar Mk II.

Detail changes included a new throttle gate plate and new boost gauge to be incorporated immediately, with further changes when components became available, including modifications to the fuel system. A new radiator and oil cooler were added to allow unrestricted use in tropical climates – on the Mk I, pilots had to exercise care when climbing not to exceed coolant and oil temperatures – along with tropical filters and a new airscrew.

The new airscrew was almost the death of Menzies during a test flight on one of the second-batch Mk II aircraft, N4043, as he explained in his interview with Brian Robinson:

> We had a twenty degree range Rotol airscrew for the first year, and in production this air screw was given an increase in pitch, which at high speeds in the dive altered the airflow over the tail, which reintroduced this rudder instability. I was doing a dive on Sunday afternoon, it was the 2nd February, 1941, and the elevators joined in with what is known as 'flutter' in general. This increased. It was a very steep terminal velocity dive, and was quite beyond my strength to control the elevators or the rudder. The tail broke off from the fuselage leaving no controls at the back of the aircraft at all. The back end came up quickly in what was known as a 'bunt' and the speed at that time was 410 mph. The tail coming up, the wings were swept backwards, the engine went out of its mounting, and I went through the Sutton harness, and the breaking strain on a Sutton harness was supposed to be something in excess of a ton.[liv]

Menzies was thrown out of the disintegrating Fulmar at around 8,000 ft. He tumbled through the air until, no more than 1,000 ft above the ground, miraculously, his parachute opened. He must have regained consciousness enough to pull the ripcord.

Perhaps mercifully, he retained little or no memory of the crash. The remaining sections of N4043 littered the Cheshire countryside. They bore silent testament to the violence of the aerodynamic instability Duncan had run into at 400 mph. The tail section, which had ripped off at the leading edge of the tailplane, sat upside down and surrounded by debris, the rudder was missing, the torque-tube fractured, and the elevators buckled as if they were tinplate. The main fuselage section was also found upside down. It looked almost intact ahead of the crumpled edges where the tail had ripped free, but the forward end was a tangled mess of wreckage. The wings had sheared off, leaving the stub wings attached but wrenched horribly out of shape. A section of one wing lay in another field, skin peeled away from the ribs like paper. The engine was half-buried, with one propeller blade sticking out of the earth and the shredded remains of the nose laying behind.

The breaking up of the Fulmar had happened within sight of Ringway. Menzies wrote: 'Charlie Thomas ... who is buried in Ringway churchyard packed my parachute for

The tail of Fairey Fulmar N4043 where it came to rest in a field outside Manchester, after shearing off the aircraft during a terminal velocity dive. (Menzies family collection)

The main fuselage section of the Fairey Fulmar N4043 after breaking up in flight. As is apparent here, the wings and tail section broke away. The force that ripped the aircraft to pieces threw Menzies out of the cockpit. (Menzies family collection)

12 years. On Sunday afternoon the 2nd of February 1941 he watched it open at 1,000 feet after a Fulmar I had on test disintegrated on me at 8,000 ft.' Duncan never forgot the debt of gratitude he owed Charlie Thomas, who he had always admired, recognising a fellow perfectionist. Thomas worked at, and later became foreman of the Fairey paint shop, which was opposite the flight test shed. Parachute packing for test pilots was just one of his responsibilities, and probably not a particularly prominent one, but it was one he performed diligently and professionally. The incident created an even closer bond with Thomas, and Menzies presented him with a silver tankard engraved with the words, 'Charles Thomas. To remind him of his part in the events of February 2nd 1941. Duncan Menzies,' in appreciation of his efforts, and every year, on the anniversary of the crash, the two men would meet for a drink at The Romper pub, just outside Ringway airport. When Thomas, who had no family, died, he left his worldly goods to Duncan.

Charlie Thomas, who worked in the Fairey Aviation paint shop, always packed Menzies' parachute. To thank him for his diligence in packing the parachute that saved his life, Duncan presented Thomas with this inscribed silver tankard. (© Matthew Willis)

'I was somewhat sick after the incident in 1941 and Sam Moseley ... had the unenviable task of continuing the trials which I had left off,'[iv] Duncan added, with typical understatement and concern for his fellow test pilot.

While he was convalescing, N1854 was converted to Mk II standard. It has sometimes been called the prototype Mk II, but in fact production Mk IIs began to appear some time before N1854 was converted. It simply made sense to bring the first Fulmar up to the standard of the machines then leaving the production line, especially with the loss of N4043. (In fact, the conversion to Mk II standard could be applied to any Mk I, and field kits were issued for just this purpose.)

The first flight after N1854's modification took place on 31 May 1941. It suffered an engine failure and was repaired in July.

In the meantime, further orders for Fulmars had been placed by the Admiralty, and in the end 600 were built. All but a few had been completed by the end of 1942, by which time new aircraft had slowed to a trickle. The Fairey Stockport test pilots were busier than ever though. An adjoining section of the Heaton Chapel factory was opened in 1938 as the Errwood Park Air Ministry 'Shadow Factory', run by Fairey, to licence-build Bristol Beaufighters and, slightly later, Handley Page Halifaxes. The Fleet Air Arm replaced the Fulmar as a fleet fighter at the end of 1942, although a number of modifications, such as a switch to .50in machine guns, the addition of an external fuel tank and the development of a night-fighter variant, had kept test aircraft occupied.

Duncan also had family life to keep him grounded and give him something to focus on when the work threatened to become overwhelming, even though he doubtless didn't get to see Scott and the children as often as he would have liked. Still, as the threat of German raids receded, the family was able to move nearer, to Knutsford, and in 1941 a third child, Peter, was born.

Chapter 12

Beaufighters and Barracudas, 1942–44

Duncan had made a couple of flights in a Beaufighter before his Fulmar crash – he actually made the first flight of a Fairey-built Beaufighter, taking up T4623 for its initial hop on 23 December 1940 – and this type started to form a major part of his responsibilities on his return to flight in May. The following month, Duncan made his first flight in a new Fairey type earmarked for production at Heaton Chapel. This was the Barracuda torpedo and dive bomber, which would begin series production in spring 1942. Duncan and his team expected to be heavily involved in developing the aircraft for use by the Fleet Air Arm, as they had with the Fulmar. Menzies flew the prototype, P1767, for 15 minutes on 11 June with Major Barlow, the Stockport factory's general manager, as passenger. At this point P1767 still had a low-set tailplane – the only Barracuda to be configured this way – and was due to go back into the Hayes factory to have a redesigned high tail fitted. The low-set tail suffered from buffeting when the flaps were deployed, which was an unacceptable characteristic for a carrier aircraft.

The majority of 1941, and the early part of 1942, was spent test-flying Fulmars and Beaufighters, with a number of reconditioned Battles reconfigured for training roles also making an appearance, as well as the odd Swordfish. The activity was largely 15–20-minute check-out flights, with numerous flights a day, often as many as eight. It must have been exhausting.

Menzies flew the second prototype Barracuda, P1770, on 30 January 1942. The majority of development flying had been done by the team at Great West, but as production neared more work on the type was coming to Ringway. The first production aircraft came off the Stockport production line in April 1942.

This Barracuda had a troubled birth, and although it would eventually prove to be extremely effective in service, had a number of flaws that had to be laboriously worked out. Sadly, the aircraft was rushed into service against Menzies' advice. Duncan's log book reveals that a great deal of time was spent with the first two production Mk I Barracudas, P9642 and P9643, from April to July 1942, working on the aircraft's controls.

Menzies flew the first production Barracuda Mk I, P9642, on 2 April 1942, in a 30-minute flight from Ringway. Early tests concentrated on the undercarriage retraction mechanism. Menzies flew P9642 repeatedly during April and May, most often with the object of studying the aircraft's controls, then focussing on lateral control and trim. The second production Mk I, P9643, was taken up by Menzies for its initial flight on 16 May, and the third production aircraft arrived at the end of June.

Menzies and his team at Ringway, Moseley and Eyskens, as well as others recruited to help with the workload, worked on the aircraft's controls; (modifications being introduced included a revised hood after problems were discovered with the initial type, which could jam open due to the pressure of the airflow). The Fairey Stockport team also contributed to some of the aerodynamic puzzles by flying with 'wool tuft' airflow indicators attached to the tail surfaces. The most significant issue exercising the Ringway test pilots, however, was lateral control, which was the subject of the majority of Menzies' test flights on Barracudas in the early months of the programme. This gradually gave way to work on fore-and-aft stability, and aerodynamic interference affecting the tail.

The early production aircraft had baffled Fairey engineers by exhibiting tail buffeting at low speed that had been experienced but cured on P1767. Both machines were similar in most respects to P1767 in its then-current state, so the phenomenon was puzzling. One of the aircraft had its tail replaced with one that had been more precisely manufactured, which had cured P1767's problems, but this time the change had no effect. The first two Barracuda Mk Is continued to suffer from buffeting on the glide approach, regardless of whether the flaps were up or down. The company went over the aircraft with a fine-tooth comb, sealing holes, improving aerodynamic fillets and fairing surface irregularities, all to no avail. As a result, P9642 was dispatched to the Royal Aircraft Establishment (RAE) at Farnborough to ascertain the cause of the buffeting problem and devise a cure.[lvi]

The RAE found – during aerodynamic tests with the Barracuda – that with the pilot's hood open, still air was being drawn out of the cockpit by the low pressure zone on the wing's upper surface, and was interfering with the airflow over the wing, flap and tail. The only satisfactory cure was achieved by installing an airtight bulkhead behind the pilot. This was recommended for production aircraft and Fairey introduced the modification onto the production line: the first test flight with an aircraft so fitted, P9644, was carried out at Ringway by Menzies on 9 July 1942.

Menzies, according to his younger son, Peter, risked his standing with the Fairey board of directors by insisting that the Barracuda was not ready and was unsafe for young and inexperienced pilots.[lvii] Unfortunately, all the previous delays meant that it was imperative to get the aircraft into production and avoid further delays once aircraft were being built. This meant that any substantial redesigns of any part of the aircraft were out of the question, so Menzies and his team had to work with the factory to implement what improvements they could.

In the midst of this difficult period, Fairey was hit by a tragedy. Chief Test Pilot Chris Staniland, the man who had recruited Duncan and led the test-flying operation at Great West since the mid-1930s, was killed when the prototype Fairey Firefly crashed. The reason, it was eventually discovered, was distressingly trivial. 'Colin Evans, who was at Great West, finally provided the evidence by belly landing a Firefly at Hatfield Bridge Flats some time later,' Menzies recalled – Evans had lost much of the fabric from the elevators. 'A new form of stitch had been introduced to fix the fabric to the ribs of the elevators (and other parts). It was not a success and Chris must have lost rather more fore and aft control than Colin was left with.'[18] He added, 'Chris should not, like many others, have died when he did.'[lviii]

The first Barracuda Mk II, P9667, was flown from Ringway by Menzies on 8 December 1942. This was the definitive early production model with a more powerful engine. It joined the group of Barracudas being tested by Fairey for a range of aspects, but largely lateral control. (Notably, towards the end of the month, flight tests began to include checks on the level of carbon monoxide in the aircraft's interior.)

In that month, Fairey Stockport's remaining communication aircraft, Stinson Reliant G-AEOR, was impressed into military service. (Hornet Moth G-ADND had been impressed at the beginning of the war). At the same time, the need for a communications aircraft was higher than ever. Fairey's main production facilities, split as they were between Hayes and Stockport, 100 miles apart, relied on good liaison between sites. Furthermore, the company now belonged to several 'production groups'. These were networks of manufacturers working on a single type to minimise the consequences of damage to a factory. Fairey belonged to the Beaufighter, Barracuda and later the Halifax groups.

This may have spurred the Fairey Stockport team to look anew at the first Fulmar, N1854, which by now was doing little. The Fulmar could cruise at over 200 mph – twice the speed of the company's previous 'hack' aircraft – and could comfortably manage the trip between Great West aerodrome and Ringway in less than an hour. It had good range, room for a passenger and was familiar to the company's pilots. Moreover, Menzies was beginning to wind down his long career as a test pilot. Around this time he took on the role

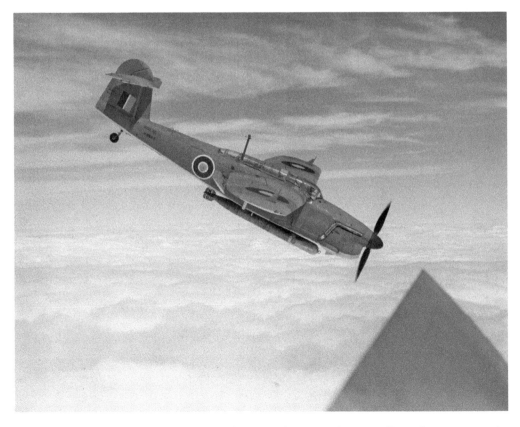

Fairey Barracuda P9667 was the first production Mk II aircraft. It was flown from Ringway by Duncan Menzies on 8 December 1942, and, complete with torpedo, took part in a photoshoot by renowned photographer Charles E. Brown. (Author's/Menzies family collection)

of Service and Liaison with the Fleet Air Arm, and this was becoming a more significant part of his work. The Fleet Air Arm then had three Fairey types (Swordfish, Albacore and Fulmar) in service, and was shortly to gain the Barracuda torpedo/dive-bomber, and then the Firefly reconnaissance fighter, so the work had considerable importance. The liaison role involved frequent travel to Royal Navy shore stations where Fairey aircraft were based. From this time, N1854 became known at Faireys simply as 'Duncan's aircraft'. 'He loved it,' his son Peter later said. 'It was his favourite aeroplane.'

On 28 February 1943, N1854's long career as Fairey's 'runabout' began when Menzies ferried Group Captain Frederick Kirk to RNAS Stretton. Kirk was an experienced naval aviator who had been appointed by the Air Ministry to oversee the Barracuda production group, and was dubbed by Sir Richard Fairey as the 'manager, critic, father, mother and nurse' to the Barracuda programme.

For much of the rest of the Second World War, Menzies flew N1854 between Ringway and Great West, and a number of RN airfields, including a number of flights carrying Kirk to stations such as Crail, where Barracuda aircrew training took place.

For all the troubles experienced by the Barracuda programme, the production aircraft had many good qualities. Test crews noted that, 'At weights up to 12,000 lb this aircraft is quite easy and pleasant to fly.'[lix] The pilots found that the aircraft's manoeuvrability compared well with that of the Swordfish and that it was greatly superior to that aircraft in speed, rate of climb and comfort. Mock dogfights with fighter aircraft were conducted, and the Barracuda proved that it could be manoeuvred vigorously in self-defence. In dives, glides and approaches the Barracuda was assessed as quite satisfactory. A series of minor failures and difficulties had been experienced during the testing phase, but few aircraft types attained service readiness without such snags.

However, in 1943 a series of serious and sometimes fatal accidents began to blight the work-up into squadron service. During this process several aircraft were lost from both frontline units, generally during torpedo practice. The incidents were thought to occur during tight turns following recovery from a dive – exactly the kind of evasive manoeuvre that would occur after a torpedo run on a heavily armed ship. The A&AEE and the RAE therefore launched investigations into the possible causes.

Fairey, through the experience their test-flying team at Ringway had gained, had ideas about what might have been behind the crashes, and passed these on to the test establishments. RAE test pilot Captain Eric 'Winkle' Brown recalled the input Duncan Menzies and his team had in diagnosing the problem:

Before the Admiralty handed over, they were aware of the fatal crashes, and asked if they knew of any good reason why. They made several suggestions, and really pointed the finger at the use of the flaps, or the dive-brake flaps in fact, and this put us on the road which we already suspected anyway was the trouble. Duncan must have been involved.[lx]

The RAE's findings were similar to those of the A&AEE, with the added knowledge that the combination of the flaps reverting to normal position and excessive rudder deflection could cause the aircraft to flick inverted. Captain Brown's account of his hair-raising test flights in which this was established is well documented.[lxi] Other difficulties such as fin-stalling during a dive were discovered during the two establishments' investigations. Armed with this knowledge, after July 1943 the number of crashes decreased dramatically – though the problems did not abate entirely. Several aircraft were seen to lose their wings in a dive, a fault that was suspected to be the result of locking pins of insufficient strength. Both this and, to a degree, the handling problems were exacerbated by the Barracuda's weight growth throughout the project. By the time the Mk II went into production, it was rather more heavily loaded and stressed than Marcelle Lobelle and his team had originally anticipated. This had an inevitable impact on components and the main structure, particularly the wing spars and fuselage frames 10 and 11.

On 4 August 1943, with the aircraft finally on the front line, Menzies flew a 'press demonstration, torpedo load' at Ringway in Barracuda P9667. No doubt a great deal of information was embargoed, but with a great deal of negative publicity about the aircraft already in the public domain, the demonstration helped to emphasise the aircraft's capabilities.

The summer and early autumn of 1943 was in fact Menzies 'last hurrah' as the lead test pilot at Stockport, focussing his experience and efforts almost exclusively on Barracuda production testing. Afterwards, his Fleet Air Arm liaison role occupied most of his time. Menzies' experience as a test pilot proved crucial during his various flights to Fleet Air Arm units, as he was able to help with 'rogue' aircraft that were not behaving as they should, and the units could not diagnose the cause.

Another image from the photoshoot of Barracuda P9667, also taken from a Barracuda. (Author's/Menzies family collection)

Part 3

A Farewell to Wings

The machine does us honour. But without men, the machine is dead. He needs a soul. It is we who have formed his character, drawn his nerve to obedience, made his intelligence lucid and quick, his will, calm and tenacious.

Jean du Plessis de Grenédan

Chapter 13

Liaison to the Fleet Air Arm, 1944–45

Fairey was aware of the reputational problems that had grown up around the Barracuda. The company perhaps felt that an experienced and trusted pilot, who could go quickly to Fleet Air Arm units and discuss any incipient problems in their own language, and feed them back to the factory quickly and accurately, would prevent such problems arising with other aircraft. There was also the fact that problems with the Barracuda had not really started until the aircraft had entered service, so forging a link between the factory test pilots and the customer could help to ensure the latter was aware of all the quirks and tricks of that particular type, especially during its service trials.

The test pilot, Captain Eric 'Winkle' Brown, who was with No. 778 Naval Air Squadron, Service Trials Unit in 1943, remembered Duncan's input during this period:

With Faireys being a naval aeroplane manufacturer, we saw quite a bit of Duncan, plus at Farnborough, and out in the field, so to speak.

Mainly he paid occasional visits up to what was called the Service Trials Unit, initially based at Arbroath in Scotland, and then after a year, about 1942, 1943, it moved to Crail, on the northern tip of the Firth of Forth. He came up whenever a new Fairey aircraft was allocated to us. The job of the Service Trials Unit was to take first time new naval aircraft onboard carriers to check out their deck-landing characteristics, and Duncan always took an interest in that. He often in fact came onto the carriers. He would come on, be flown on by the Navy and stay for the trials, which were usually a couple of days. And indeed he used to come onto the escort carriers – the Americans were sending escort carriers to us very rapidly, one after the other, by about 1942, and Duncan often came on those because the main aircraft we used for them were the Swordfish and Albacore and then two fighters as well as the others, and ... the Barracuda. But in the earlier ones, the first time I met him, I was flying the Fulmar. And later on, of course, he was involved, or he came to the trials, anyway, of the Firefly. He was involved in quite a host of aeroplanes really. I don't know if he was involved with the Firefly but he was certainly taking an interest in it as he attended the trials.

I think even if Duncan wasn't directly involved, such as with the Firefly, he would seek any excuse to be there because he enjoyed coming with the Navy. Like another one, Joe Smith of Supermarine loved coming on the trials because he could just enjoy a couple of days with the Navy, jollification in the wardroom. I think Duncan was of the same stamp.[lxii]

As well as wardroom jollity, Menzies undoubtedly took a keen interest in the way the aircraft behaved operating from carriers, looking for information that might help the factory, or assist pilots flying the machines. The problems with the Barracuda, and later the Firefly, which killed no fewer than three Fairey test pilots and one from the A&AEE, meant there could be absolutely no complacency.

In December 1944, Menzies' liaison role, and the problems with the Firefly, took him all the way to South Asia. On Boxing Day he flew in an Avro York to Ceylon to help the Fleet Air Arm investigate Firefly crashes. The exact problem is not clear, and there don't seem to have been any fatal accidents over this period – the last aircrew killed in a Firefly had been two members of No. 1770 Squadron, who died in a crash at Heathfield in October. Evidently the difficulties were serious enough to bring Duncan thousands of miles to assist. It was almost certainly No. 1770 Squadron that was the cause of the investigation. This unit had been the first front-line Firefly Squadron to equip with the type, and sailed for the Far East in late 1944, stopping at Puttalam, Ceylon, on 10 December and carrying out intensive weapons training, particularly with rocket projectiles. Menzies arrived on 29 December, and in January carried out various flights in Firefly Mk I DK422 – relatively long flights of an hour and 30 or 40 minutes, going between Colombo Racecourse, Coimbatore, and China Bay, Trincomalee. (Coincidentally, Val Bennett, who would later marry Duncan's daughter Mary Ann, was then in the Indian Ocean as an Observer with No. 1772 Squadron, the third Firefly Squadron to form, aboard HMS *Ruler*, on their way to join 1770 aboard HMS *Indefatigable* for the final battle in the Far East.)

Menzies returned to England at the beginning of February 1945. It seems that 'his' aircraft, Fulmar N1854, had been little used, as his log book entry for 22 June records 'Test flight. A/C Rejuvenated', suggesting the aircraft needed some work to render it fit for duty. After that had been achieved, the Fulmar once again became his chief transport.

By now, the war in Europe was all but over. Orders for aircraft were even being cancelled and scaled back, though development of newer and improved types continued. Duncan's liaison work continued, and he continued working on the Barracuda to an extent – mainly on the more powerful and larger Mk V variant, which promised to finally overcome the aircraft's shortcomings. The Mk V was sadly too late to see action, and orders for all but around thirty were cancelled.

Chapter 14

Fireflies and Firefly Trainers, 1945–52

With the fighting over in Europe, and then the Far East, Duncan's visit to Fleet Air Arm stations were scaled back dramatically. The company's attention began to turn to its legacy, as huge numbers of naval aircraft were stored, scrapped or just pushed off of aircraft carriers into the sea. Fairey was not unaware of the danger of losing parts of the company's, and the country's, heritage in the rush to dispose of vast numbers of surplus aircraft. Already there were no Fairey-built Swordfish available for preservation, so the company had to acquire the Blackburn-built LS326. Menzies collected the aircraft from Sherburn-in-Elmet in January 1946.[19] That year Fairey applied to have N1854 placed on the civil register, and it was given the registration G-AIBE. The aircraft would still earn its keep, but was increasingly seen as a 'heritage asset'.

With the end of the war, Menzies had a new cause to champion. He had seen firsthand how front-line aircraft had gained dramatically in power and performance – aircraft entering service with the Fleet Air Arm around that time included the Firefly Mk IV, Seafire Mk 47 and Hawker Sea Fury, which all had powerplants of over 2,000 hp – while training aircraft were generally similar to those in use at the beginning of the war. There was clearly a need for a training aircraft that filled the gap and allowed pilots to acclimatise to a much more powerful machine without having to jump from a 700 hp 'advanced' trainer to fly solo in a 2,000 hp single-seater. At the end of the war the Admiralty began to express a desire for a deck-landing trainer of similar performance to the latest service types. Menzies visited the Admiralty and persuaded the Director of Air Warfare and the Director of Air Organisation of Training that the Firefly could be readily adapted to this purpose (cost-effectively, too, as the Admiralty already owned many now-obsolescent Firefly Mk Is).[lxiii] He then persuaded the Fairey board to take it on as a private venture. If Duncan was right, interest would not be limited to the Fleet Air Arm, and not just to naval air services.

In the Firefly Trainer, the space formerly occupied by the Observer's cockpit was filled by a second, fully fitted-out pilot's cockpit, the floor 12 inches above that of the forward cockpit. This afforded the instructor an excellent view and required relatively little modification to the structure of the aircraft. A Firefly then at Stockport for repairs, MB750, was earmarked for conversion as the prototype, while another Mk I, Z2033, was mocked up with the revised rear fuselage shape for aerodynamic testing. The former first flew in May 1946 and the latter in June, both with Sam Moseley making the first flight as Menzies was no longer strictly a test pilot. This did not deter him, however, and

Fairey developed the Firefly Trainer as a private venture after the Second World War to help pilots adapt to increasingly powerful and high-performance aircraft entering service. Menzies flew the company's demonstrator, MB750, to numerous operational air stations in the UK and overseas in the late 1940s. (Author's collection)

he flew MB750 (wearing 'Class B' registration F-1) on 2 July, testing the handling and carrying out carbon monoxide tests to ensure that the rear cockpit did not suffer from an excessive build up of the gas. All was well, so he flew the aircraft to Heston for a two-day demonstration to senior officers of the Fleet Air Arm's Training Branch on 15–16 August. At the end of the month, the aircraft went to Boscombe Down for testing by the A&AEE.

On 10 September Duncan collected F-1 from his former employers and flew it to Radlett for the Society of British Aircraft Manufacturers (SBAC) air show, where Sam Moseley demonstrated it, before it went back to Boscombe to finish the brief tests. Then, in October, Menzies toured the prototype around various operational aerodromes – Lossiemouth, Milltown, Donibristle, Squires Gate, where his friend Ken MacEwan had died in 1941. The Advanced Flying School (RNAS Hinstock), the Navy's Operational Flying School (Lossiemouth), the Deck Landing Training Station (Milltown), and the School of Naval Warfare (RNAS St Merryn) all had a chance to try out the trainer.

Despite all the work put in, a chance arose that the Firefly Trainer would be elbowed out. A separate programme by Vickers Supermarine, proposing an adaptation of the Spitfire, had gained some momentum, and the two rival projects were forced to battle it out. W. Harrison describes the good-natured confrontation in his book *Fairey Firefly: The Operational Record*: 'So, in the latter half of 1946 Duncan Menzies found himself sitting at the Admiralty opposite Geoffrey Quill of Vickers Supermarine, in the same office, at the same time and becoming good friends as they tried to convince the Minister that their aeroplane was best!'[lxiv]

In reality there can have been little doubt over the greater suitability of the Firefly. It offered much better visibility for the instructor, was considerably more robust and its wide-track undercarriage designed for deck landing dramatically cut down the chances of landing accidents.

In December 1946, Menzies toured the prototype around various operational and training sites overseas. He left Hendon on 4 December, flying to Toussus-le-Noble, France, then to Les Mureaux, where naval test pilots flew the aircraft. He then returned to Manston via Buc, before turning around and heading to Valkenborg, home of the Dutch Navy's Operational Flying School.

In a demonstration to Flight shortly after the tour, Duncan explained the value of the machine, which had only been reinforced by his tour:

> Mr Menzies confirmed on his travels that a relatively high percentage of mishaps occur as a result of incorrect handling on the ground, by pupils unaccustomed to the 'feel' of modern high-performance fighters with relatively high wing-loadings. An average pupil may need four hours or more to familiarise himself with a modern fighter, and expensive accidents are not infrequent.[lxv]

Two of the original four cannon were retained for weapons training, and underwing stores, such as bombs and rockets, could be fitted as with the operational aircraft.

The venture was a complete success and resulted in thirty-four T Mk 1 and fifty-seven T Mk 2 variants being produced, all converted from former fighters, for Britain, Canada and the Netherlands. This project was typical of Menzies, whose thoughts were never far from the need to make inexperienced pilots' lives easier and safer. Furthermore, when the Australian Navy purchased Firefly Mk 5s, Fairey Stockport produced three kits to convert aircraft locally to Trainer specification (known as T Mk 5), and a fourth kit was manufactured to the same pattern in Australia.

With the Firefly Trainer work in hand, Duncan reacquainted himself with Fulmar G-AIBE in preparation of resuming his normal service and liaison work. On 22 January 1947 he made a test flight in connection with the application for a civilian Certificate of Airworthiness. This was the first flight under the aircraft's civilian identity, but Duncan's log book notes, 'Alias N1854 prototype and last surviving Fulmar.' This is not quite true – Fulmars were present at the Balado Bridge dump as late as 1953, but undoubtedly at the time, any other surviving Fulmars were likely to be in poor condition and would have had no hope of preservation.

On its transfer to civilian flight, G-AIBE was painted in an attractive scheme of Fairey's in-house colours; silver, with the spine and registration letters in dark blue. The need for communication between Fairey's sites would continue – this was even more necessary since the company had established a factory at Heston in 1944, and would also gain a presence at White Waltham in Berkshire. In fact, the Menzies family moved from Knutsford to a house near White Waltham in this period, though Duncan was actually based at Hayes.

The first Fulmar also found use assisting Fairey's commercial enterprises. G-AIBE evidently made an effective camera-ship, as numerous flights were made in the late 1940s and early '50s carrying out air-to-air photography of aircraft Fairey hoped to sell.

The first Fairey Fulmar, N1854, re-purposed as the company's communications aircraft, was put on the civil register after the Second World War as G-AIBE and was painted in Fairey house colours of dark blue and silver. It is seen here after roll-out in its new scheme. (Menzies family collection)

These included various light aircraft marketed by Fairey under the Tipsy brand, such as the Belfair, Trainer and Primer, and military aircraft including the prototype Gannet anti-submarine aeroplane. Several of these photography sorties saw Menzies flying the famed aerial photographer Charles E. Brown. On Sunday 27 May, Duncan gave a display of the Fulmar at the opening of Fairey Aviation's own flying club at White Waltham. Flight noted that Menzies 'showed what the Fulmar could do,' impressing with its manoeuvrability, even if 'one could not help feeling what a pity it was that the Fulmar was always underpowered'. In addition to the Fulmar, Sam Moseley demonstrated a Barracuda, Gordon Slade a Spearfish (a stillborn Barracuda replacement) and 'Freddie' Dixon flew the company Swordfish, while Peter Twiss aerobatted a Firefly Mk 4.

After the war, the Royal Australian Navy and the Royal Canadian Navy, which had operated substantially as part of the British Royal Navy, agreed with the Admiralty to establish their own naval air arms, based around new light fleet aircraft carriers now surplus to RN requirements. Both chose Fairey Firefly fighters as part of the air groups, so Menzies was to be heavily involved in liaison with the customers and helping the Australians and Canadians adapt to their new aircraft. In the same period, the Dutch Navy purchased the carrier HMS *Venerable*, renamed HNLMS *Karel Doorman*, intending to fly their Firefly aircraft from it.

The Royal Canadian Navy (RCN) had taken delivery of the Colossus-class light fleet carrier HMCS *Warrior* in 1946 and operated it with Firefly FR Mk Is and Supermarine Seafire F. Mk XVs. *Warrior* was not entirely suitable for the conditions in which it had to operate, so a second carrier, the Majestic-Class HMCS *Magnificent*, was prepared, being fitted out properly for colder waters, and by early 1948, was ready to be commissioned at Belfast. At the same time, No. 825 Squadron was re-equipping with the new Firefly Mk 4 variant, and Menzies flew some modification sets to Belfast on 21 May in de Havilland Dragon Rapide G-AKJE. While here, he was invited to a wardroom party to celebrate the commissioning.

For Duncan's family, this visit was chiefly notable for the acquisition of a number of ducks, which for a while improved their quality of life during a time of rationing and post-war austerity. Mary Ann recalled that:

> There were two drakes called Warrior and Magnificent, and half a dozen ducks that all came back from Belfast – the Navy had had them swimming in a tarpaulin filled with water. Quite how they became our father's property in not any clearer. The ducks were part of an RN party, and the Navy didn't know what to do with them after the party, they were therefore given to him and he flew them home in Fairey's Rapide.

Peter added that:

> These were days when food rationing was a daily problem. I have no memory of actually being hungry but I do remember the importance of the ration book and how concerned my mother was about getting food for her children. I remember her pleasure when Daddy came back from one of these visits with the khaki Campbell ducks that he had won, named after aircraft carriers, whose eggs we ate. We never ate the ducks because they were stolen before we got there! We also had a pig later but I think that rationing must have eased in the early fifties before we ate it.[lxvi]

The relationship with the RCN was an important one for Fairey, and Duncan made a number of visits to Canada in relation to that. 'In the late forties or early fifties my father made several visits – not short, six weeks or so – to Canada,' Peter recalled. 'I remember going one day with my mother to meet him at Southampton coming back from one of these visits on the *Mauretania*.'

It does not seem that Duncan's next trip to see a customer was as rewarding in terms of livestock as the Belfast visit, but was all part of the 'hands-on' approach with customers. On 2–3 June 1948 Menzies flew G-AKJE from Lympne to Valkenborg, concerning Firefly Trainers for HNLMS *Karel Doorman*.

The third customer in this period for Fairey Firefly aircraft was the Royal Australian Navy, which had bought Majestic-class carrier HMS *Terrible*, to be renamed HMAS *Sydney*. Although *Sydney* was commissioned in December 1948, the carrier had not yet been completed. Menzies paid a visit to the ship while the air group was still working up in Scotland, flying to Donibristle on 25 February, then to Arbroath on 28 February and returning to White Waltham on 3 March 1949. The following month he flew to Australia and spent a year there, assisting with the assembly and entry into service of

Menzies was responsible for liaison with the Royal Canadian Navy during its purchase of Fairey Firefly strike fighters. He is seen here with a Commander of the RCN and his wife, and Jock Cunningham, First Lieutenant of the Royal Yacht, enjoying a cocktail party aboard the yacht. (Menzies family collection)

No. 816 Squadron's Firefly Mk 5 aircraft. Menzies' help preparing the carrier's Firefly crews was clearly appreciated, and he was presented with a solid silver napkin ring engraved with the ship's name. He returned home in April 1950.

The work was of great importance – HMAS *Sydney* was called up for United Nations service in the Korean War. She remained on station from September 1951 to January 1952, flying through highly challenging winter conditions to keep up sustained attacks on North Korean positions. The Fireflies flew around 750 sorties before *Sydney* was relieved by HMS *Glory*. Australia purchased over 100 Fireflies, and the type was a stalwart of the country's Fleet Air Arm in the late 1940s and '50s.

On his return from Australia, Duncan once again adopted the Fulmar G-AIBE as his personal transport. The first Fulmar was also increasingly a living demonstration of the company's heritage. Often the Fulmar would fly in joint displays with the company's Swordfish LS326, now registered G-AJVH and painted in the 'reverse' of G-AIBE's colours. The Fulmar was often to be seen during the 1950s at Royal Aeronautical Society garden parties at White Waltham and Wisley, and was also displayed at Farnborough on the 50th anniversary of the RFC's formation, the final Air Day at RNAS Ford, and many other events. One notable flight in the Fulmar took place on 14 November 1950, from White Waltham to the 'Martlesham area'. Menzies' log book records a passenger, 'V.S.P.'. In all probability this was the mortal remains of Vivian Steel Parker, one of the few contemporaries of Menzies during his RAF career who had survived the war. Parker had flown and played golf with Duncan at the A&AEE, and later gone back to command the establishment. Menzies took up G-AIBE that day to scatter his ashes. Peter explained that Parker was,

> ... an Australian pilot who was also at Martlesham. His nickname was 'Lovely' Parker and they played golf together. And after Lovely Parker's death, my father spread his ashes, from an aeroplane, over the golf club. The ashes were contained in a sort of hessian bag, I think it had 'Midland Bank, £10 silver' written on it. And my father must have just tipped it over the side of the aeroplane. I can still remember as a child not being allowed to play with 'Lovely' Parker's bag, which hung from a nail on the roof of my father's workshop.[lxvii]

But Menzies and N1854's relationship was soon to come to an end, at least in terms of the Fulmar being his personal mount. On 12 February 1952, he took G-AIBE up for a 25-minute flight around White Waltham. It was Menzies' last, and marked his retirement from flying. Menzies was forty-seven – not old by any standards, even for piloting, but flying had evidently lost a lot of its shine in the increasingly crowded skies over the UK in the 1950s. Peter recalled Duncan telling him that flight was no longer the carefree business it had been in the 1920s. An exchange between Menzies and Air Traffic Control may have been the last straw – evidently, the controller had tried to insist Duncan hold at an altitude the ten-year-old Fulmar could never have reached. It had been a quarter of a century since that Avro 504K had lumbered into the air over Egypt guided by an excited young man who had the whole sky to play with, but it was now bounded with radar, direction-finding beams, beacons, and endless rules. It was a good time to release the controls.

Chapter 15

Retirement, 1952–97

The liaison role involved a certain amount of pressing the flesh and socialising, which Menzies had always taken to naturally. Photographs from post-war functions show him in black tie, surrounded by figures in uniforms weighed down with gold braid and medals. In one of them, Menzies is sitting with a Commander RCN and the First Officer of the Royal Yacht, while the Canadian officer's wife feeds a piglet with a baby's bottle. Others are marked with the stamp of The Dorchester, and one the Celebrity Club Sydney, which leaves space for autographs. His companions have signed the card with messages for Scott, back in England – one reassures her that, 'Duncan has been a good boy he has been to bed every night at 8 a.m.' Mary Ann says of the photographs, 'It looks as though my parents lived a most glamorous life, which wasn't at all the case!'[lxviii] Indeed, the opulence that was sometimes seen must have been in stark contrast to the austerity of 1940s and '50s England. Duncan was never paid an extravagant sum for his services. Indeed, in the 1970s his company pension suffered from the ravages of inflation and threatened to leave him and Scott in financial difficulties in their later years. Gordon Slade, who followed Duncan as a test pilot with Faireys, helped rectify the situation, but it must have seemed scant reward for the efforts and risk Menzies underwent for King and Company.

Although he was no longer flying, Duncan's knowledge and experience was still of great value to Fairey Aviation. In the post-war years, Duncan acted as the host at Fairey's enclosure at the SBAC show, responsible for entertaining industry figures and potential customers of Fairey products. He performed this role until Westland's takeover of Fairey in 1960.

While Duncan's relationship with Sir Richard Fairey could not be described as close, it nevertheless went beyond that of employer and employee. Sir Richard invited Duncan to shoot with him at his estate every year until he died in 1956.

In May 1964, when Menzies retired from Fairey, the Managing Director, C. H. Chichester-Smith, wrote a letter of apology for missing his leaving party at the Hind's Head Hotel, Bray. The letter is, by the formal standards of the day, clearly heartfelt, and indicates how highly Duncan was thought of within the company:

> Dear Duncan,
> I am afraid I am not going to be able to get to your party tonight, and I hope you will forgive me. I am not too good at these affairs these days, but as I am quite sure that there will be so many of your friends there anyway that my absence will hardly be noticed.

A collection of Fairey test pilots at a gathering in February 1961. From left to right: Peter Twiss (World Speed Record 1956, Fairey Delta 2); Jimmy Matthews (Fairey guided weapons testing); Sam Moseley; Ron Gellatly (Fairey Rotodyne testing); John Dennis (Fairey Jet Gyrodyne testing); David Masters (Fairey Gannet testing); Duncan Menzies; Gordon Slade (Fairey Delta 1 testing, and Delta 2 record planning); and Johnny Morton (Rotodyne testing). (Menzies family collection)

I have already told you, in a previous letter, how much I appreciate all you did for the Company during your long association with it, and I am sure the warmth of your reception tonight will clearly endorse all I have said.

One of these days when we both are less involved we might have lunch together in a rather more private capacity.

All the best Duncan and I hope you will have a happy evening.

While Duncan's career in aviation was now over, his influence could still be felt in the world of test-flying. In 1954 his nephew, who had been named after him – Duncan Menzies Soutar Simpson – had taken up a role as test pilot at Hawker Aviation. Simpson is frank about the inspiration his uncle provided, and his own glittering career bears testament to Menzies' passion for aviation and test-flying. Simpson rose to become Chief Test Pilot at Hawker Siddeley, leading the test programme of the highly successful Hawk trainer. His other test programme credits include the Harrier 'jump jet', the Hunter and Sea Fury fighters.

As one generation of test pilots rose, another began to fade. The test pilot community in Britain had always been tight-knit. It had been forged in mutual risk and respect. The mortality rate for British test pilots was somewhere higher than one in four – Ken Ellis' study of British test pilots since 1910[20] covers 377 pilots, of whom 101 died in the course of their duties. In Duncan's retirement, he attended more funerals for his contemporaries. Harry Alexander Purvis retired from test-flying but died at the too young age of sixty-one in 1966. Mike Lithgow, Supermarine and BAC test pilot, was killed when the prototype One-Eleven airliner crashed in 1963.

In the 1980s, there was at least a glimmer of recognition for Duncan's service, though less for his years of test-flying and work with the Fleet Air Arm than the simple fact of his being the first person to land an aeroplane at Manchester Ringway. The year 1988 marked the fiftieth anniversary of the official opening of the airport (although of course Fairey had been using it for some time before that) and Duncan was invited to take part in *The Airport 50 Show*, a live event on BBC television to mark the occasion.

On 8 June 1988, Duncan wrote to Sam Moseley, describing his experiences at the broadcast:

Dear Sam,
I have to apologise for being so long in keeping in touch with you but I have an excuse and many of them.

I have been going around in circles for the last three weeks and will be for some time to come. I doubt if we will be into this house for another 4-5 weeks. The bathroom and kitchen are not yet started or floored yet.

You will be more interested in Ringway than anything here. I told the BBC that my wife was not having me at my age making the journey by myself and I agreed with her, in no time it was fixed that Sandy should look after me which was what Scott and I wanted.

The BBC was on the ball and 10 mins after take off I was sitting behind the captain of a 737 with a glass of whisky in my hand. They were a grand crew and I had 50 mins up front until engine shut down.

Good vision on the approach to the main runway NE to SW. We were taken to a hangar (about 4 p.m. arrival) ... until 7 p.m. when the stage came to life a bit. There was an Avro, I forget the name, a contra prop E.W. version of the Lincoln[21], in the hangar with crew from Lossiemouth. Discussion with them helped to pass the time.

From 7 p.m. until 10 p.m. was a kind of variety show with a good band, a comic called Bernie something who worked damned hard. Dancers and singers.

Between items individuals were interviewed. The first was a driver of one [of the] big CAT earth movers for his memories, I thought he did well. 10 mins later I was faced with it and really no idea of what was required of me except that I was the first person to land an aeroplane at Ringway.

I said something ad lib but generally forgot what it was and did not feel good.

People were kind but of course they would be.

Come 10 p.m. the performers, artistes etc had a mixed dance act which included hauling a man or two out of the front seats, Sandy being one of them. Next morning I had in my room two archivists with a tape recorder 9 a.m. to 10 a.m ... I was short of speech and they were amateurs in the operation of the tape machine.

Wish you had been the target instead of me, things would have been more successful.
Regards to you both from Scott and Self.
Sandy joined in.
Yours,
Duncan

Duncan's background in engineering, and the inevitable acquaintance he had with machinery, stood him in good stead even in retirement. On one occasion in the 1970s he took issue with a motor garage for failing his car's MOT test over excessive corrosion on the brake pipes. He pressed the mechanic over the instrument that had been used to measure the depth of corrosion, eventually securing an admission that the measurement had been taken with the mechanic's thumbnail! Duncan removed the brake pipes and used sandpaper to clean off the surface corrosion, beneath which the pipes were in good condition.

According to Peter, his father 'always had a plan, and a plan B and a plan C'. He took care to pass on his interest in technical matters to his younger son by rebuilding an MG sports car with him, although he discouraged Peter from becoming a pilot. To Duncan, flying no longer symbolised freedom from the Earth and its cares.

He continued to take a keen interest in the preservation of aircraft he had been involved in the development of. He corresponded with the Strathallan Collection with regard to their Fairey Battle R3950 (now in the Royal Military Museum, Brussels, representing the Battles of the Belgian Air Force) and the Royal Navy Historic Flight, who were custodians of the former Fairey-owned Swordfish LS326, and, at the time, Firefly WB271, which had served with the Australian Fleet Air Arm. 'His' Fulmar G-AIBE kept flying with Fairey Aviation until 1962, when the company, now under the control of Westland, presented it to the Royal Navy. Duncan later heard that it had been rendered unflyable when the hydraulic system had been topped up with the wrong fluid, which blew out all the seals. In 1972, the first and last Fulmar was presented to the Fleet Air Arm Museum at Yeovilton, where it remains to this day.

Duncan and Scott moved back to Scotland, to Ross-shire, in 1965 and then to Wales in 1978, before finally moving back to Scotland to live with their eldest son, Sandy, in Aberdeenshire, where they spent the rest of their lives. Peter recalls:

My mother died in September 1995 and was cremated. My father died in May 1997, and was also cremated. They had been living on my brother Sandy's farm in Aberdeenshire and later that summer there was a memorial service at Logie Easter Burial Ground in Ross-shire, a more than two-hour drive from the farm. Sandy's friend Chris Howard, a helicopter pilot, had a Porsche and Sandy thought that it was most appropriate to use it as a high-speed hearse.

Fellow test pilots Peter Twiss and Duncan Simpson, both in attendance, no doubt approved, and Duncan himself would have too.

Epilogue: A Personal Reflection

Before I was contacted by Mary Ann Bennett in response to a request I had made for information about the Fulmar, I had heard of Duncan Menzies, but only, in all honesty, in passing. In the various histories of the Fairey Company and its products, he appears briefly. Even one or two references to his time at the A&AEE have made it into print – The Putnam's book on Blackburn Aircraft[lxix] notes that Flight Lieutenant D. Menzies picked up the first production Shark and delivered it to Martlesham, for example. But these odd references do not add up to anything like the full story of Duncan, his team at Ringway and the very great contribution to the war effort (and aviation before and after the war) that they made. It is true that most of the heroes of the heyday of British aviation are unsung, and it would be impossible to tell the full story of all of them – but that does not mean that more could not and should not be done to bring some of their stories, belatedly, to light.

When I began to learn more about Duncan, I was astonished I had not heard more of him in the general course of my studies and interest in aviation, particularly around naval aviation and the products of the Fairey Aviation Company. I had liked to think of myself as knowledgeable about these matters, and could name a string of test pilots from roughly the era in which Menzies was most active, yet he (and those of his team) had largely passed me by. Of course, many of the test pilots with the highest public profile owe that to record-breaking flights, particularly speed records. Those such as Neville Duke and Peter Twiss, even Chuck Yeager, might not have become household names were it not for their highly publicised speed records in the 1940s and '50s. The British records perhaps became more notable, coming as they did in an era when Britain's star as an aviation powerhouse was beginning to wane and records and achievements did not come as thick and fast as they had in the pre-war era (there was a period in the early 1930s when Britain held the speed, distance and altitude records at the same time, against significant competition). Even Eric 'Winkle' Brown, these days widely regarded as Britain's greatest aviator, did not gain widespread recognition outside the aviation community until the final years of his life. It may be that one-off achievements such as speed records, and even impressive career totals such as 'Winkle' Brown's records for deck landings and types flown, overshadow the most significant work of the test pilot, which is generally far less glamorous – but certainly no less important. Indeed, they may be considered more so, for they impact greatly on the performance, safety and utility of aircraft that, if all goes well, largely goes unnoticed.

The Fulmar's achievements in Fleet Air Arm service were in no small part the result of Duncan's painstaking efforts to improve it. Having been a service pilot, Menzies had a keen understanding of what the ideal characteristics of a military aircraft should be – in particular, that they should be easily manageable by inexperienced pilots. That the Fulmar was widely regarded as a straightforward but manoeuvrable machine to fly can be attributed to Duncan's abilities as a development pilot as well as to Marcelle Lobelle's design.

Chris Howard, the family friend whose Porsche served as Duncan and Scott's 'high-speed hearse', wrote:

> Duncan was a lovely man – very easy to talk to. He really loved his flying and was very modest about his achievements. I detected steel beneath the very amiable surface. It was certainly not all he could talk about. He had a love of nature and wildlife – he and I went to see huge flocks of starlings perform just before dusk a few miles from where he was then living in Scotland.[lxx]

Behind Menzies' obvious professionalism, it's easy to miss much of his life outside flying, but the few accounts I have been able to uncover reveal that he was also a very sociable man, popular and fun. 'He was a great companion in the wardroom, I can tell you that! He was a good raconteur, and he liked a jolly with the boys,' said Captain Eric Brown.[lxxi]

'Dad was a good all-round athlete which enabled him to play at all sorts of games,' wrote his daughter Mary Ann. 'Being part of teams helps one to be relaxed and make contact easily socially and he was ably backed by Mummy.' He was, of course, a devoted family man, and was married for sixty years.

Duncan was never awarded any medals for his service with the RAF, nor did he receive any civilian honours – he did not seek them, and would not have asked. A report from *Flight* during his posting to the A&AEE in 1935 encapsulates what I have learned about Menzies perfectly. It outlines how the visitor to Martlesham who 'expects be regaled with tales of how pilots dice with death, cheat the grim reaper, and flirt with disaster ... will come away unsatisfied'.[lxxii] He will, instead, 'meet the most modest, charming and skilful pilots in the world', as I feel I have, through writing this book. I hope through reading it, you will have too.

Notes

1. MacEwen rose to the rank of Squadron Leader, and was serving with No. 245 Squadron when he was killed in the crash of Bristol Blenheim L6780 while on take-off from Squires Gate, 13 April 1941.
2. In 1935, the scheme was changed so all pilots undertook basic flying training at a civilian flying school in the UK and the FTS course was shortened to six months, concentrating purely on advanced Service flying training.
3. [*sic*] – Ubee means the 'N'.
4. The most likely candidate seems to be Pilot Officer C. W. Black, who joined the RAF in May 1928, though it has not been possible to verify this.
5. Navigation over land by landmarks and checkpoints.
6. In 1932 Iraq technically became independent but was in many respects still a puppet state for the British Empire.
7. Seaplanes and flying boats were tested at the Marine Aircraft Experimental Establishment at Felixstowe.
8. Some accounts suggest the crash was fatal, but Richmond appears to have recovered and was listed in the RAF reserve in 1939.
9. Air Defence of Great Britain.
10. [*Sic*] – actually prototype K4295, rebuilt to production standard.
11. Sayer became Chief Test Pilot at Gloster when Hawkers took over that company in 1934.
12. Fairey had previously shown considerable ambition to supply fighter aircraft to the RAF as well, and its Firefly IIM almost beat the Hawker Fury in the interceptor fighter competition of 1929. Subsequently, the company concentrated on bombers.
13. Published sources differ as to where K7558 was built, where it was first flown and who first flew it. The most common variation is that the aircraft was constructed at Hayes, the only production Battle to be built there, and was flown by Chris Staniland (and other sources suggest that the first fifteen Battles were built at Hayes). I believe the confusion has arisen from the aircraft being flown to Great West a few weeks after its first flight to be demonstrated there by Staniland. Its first flight was definitely on 14 April, and Menzies' log books confirm that he flew it that day, at Barton.
14. Harker's best-known contribution to aviation was his recommendation of fitting the North American Mustang with the Rolls-Royce Merlin 60-series engine, thus creating the most effective long-range fighter of the Second World War.

15 The P.4/34 competition for a faster and more nimble light bomber than the Battle was won by Hawker with its Henley design, which used numerous Hurricane components and sub-assemblies. The requirement was cancelled after orders had been placed, with the result that hundreds of Henleys were in service as target tugs when the much slower Battles were in combat over France. Arguably both the Henley and the Fairey design would have made a more effective, and more survivable, aircraft for the Advanced Air Striking Force. The tactical strike role would eventually be fulfilled largely by fighter-bombers.

16 'An Airman's Letter To His Mother' was written by a young airman in a bomber squadron in early 1940, to be posted to his mother in the event of his death. It was published in *The Times*, printed as a leaflet and made into a short film by Powell and Pressburger.

17 Eight was an unusual number for a fighter squadron to operate in, due to the customary three-aircraft section being the standard 'unit'. Flight Lieutenant Green, in command, suffered a forced landing at Kempton Park Racecourse, hence there one aircraft being missing – my thanks to Bob Sikkel for noticing the discrepancy and for providing the extract from No. 92 Squadron's Operations Records Book to confirm.

18 A further contributory factory may have been the tendency of cockpit canopies to detach in flight and strike the tailplane, as identified by Eric 'Winkle' Brown some time later.

19 LS326 survives, and is even in flying condition, having been presented to the Royal Navy in the 1960s, and is now part of the Royal Navy Historic Flight based at Yeovilton.

20 *Testing to the Limits: British Test Pilots Since 1910*, Crecy Publishing, Vol. 1 (2015), Vol. 2 (2016).

21 This was an Avro Shackleton AEW Mk 2 – Avro being as strongly associated with Manchester as Fairey was.

References

[i]   Howard, Michael, *Review of Viscount Templewood, Empire of the Air*, New Statesman & Nation, 26 January 1957

[ii]   Paterson, Robert, via email from Peter Menzies, 29 August 2016

[iii]   Royal Air Force, *A Short History of the Royal Air Force, Chapter 2 – The Inter War Years 1919–1939*, RAF, 2005. p. 55

[iv]   Ibid., p. 59

[v]   Ubee Richard Sydney, *Imperial War Museum Oral History recording*, Catalogue number 12893 Reel 1, 1992

[vi]   Jenks, George, via email from Peter Menzies, 15 February 2013

[vii]   Nesbit-Dufort, John DSO, *Open Cockpit – Flying Pre-War Fighting And Training Aircraft*, Speed and Sports Publications 1970, p. 64

[viii]   Ibid., pp. 64–65

[ix]   Gwynn, Major General Sir Charles W. KCB, CMG, DSO, *Imperial Policing*, MacMillan and Co. 1939, p. 221

[x]   No. 45 (B) Squadron, Operations Record Book, volume 1 (National Archives AIR 27/455), p. 11

[xi]   Howard, Chris, email to the author, 19 January 2017

[xii]   No. 47 (B) Squadron, Operations Record Book, volume 1 (National Archives AIR 27/462), p. 19

[xiii]   Nesbit-Dufort, John DSO, *Open Cockpit – Flying Pre-War Fighting And Training Aircraft*, Speed and Sports Publications 1970, p. 51

[xiv]   Ibid., pp. 54–55

[xv]   No. 47 (B) Squadron, Operations Record Book, volume 1 (National Archives AIR 27/462), p. 40

[xvi]   *The Air Estimates Speech (1930)*, Flight, 21 March 1930, p. 324

[xvii]   No. 47 (B) Squadron, Operations Record Book, vol. 1 (National Archives AIR 27/462), p. 42

[xviii]   Ibid., p. 43

[xix]   Northern Times, *New Record*, 20 February 1930, reprinted 22 February 1980, Menzies family archive

[xx]   See Wheeler, Sara, *Too Close to The Sun: The Life and Times of Denys Finch Hatton*, Jonathan Cape, 2006, p. 273

[xxi]   Ibid., p. 288

xxii   *The Prince Flies Home*, Flight, 2 May 1930, p. 473

xxiii   See O'Connor, Derek, *Flying the Furrow*, The Aviation Historian Issue #1 Autumn 2012, pp. 48–57

xxiv   Gledhill, Dave, in conversation with the author, 1 February 2017

xxv   *Martlesham Dines The Industry*, Flight, 7 December 1933, p. 1241

xxvi   'Martlesham is pleased', Flight, 13 December 1929, p. 1301

xxvii   *Martlesham Dines The Industry*, Flight, 7 December 1933, p. 1241

xxviii   *An Experimental Experience – Empire Air Day Preparations: A Visit to Martlesham and Felixstowe*, Flight, 16 May 1935, p. 532

xxix   'J. Y.', *Exposed!*, Flight, 20 December 1934, p. 1345

xxx   Aeroplane and Armament Experimental Establishment, *Shark K4880 Tiger VI*, September 1936, National Archives AVIA 18/605

xxxi   *Our Air Defence: Problems of Raising the New Squadrons: The Progress Made*, Flight, 13 December 1934, p. 1323

xxxii   National Advisory Committee for Aeronautics, *Aircraft Circular No.175 Heinkel He 64c Sport Airplane (German)*, February 1933, p. 1

xxxiii   Serby, J. E. (BA), and Squire, H. B. (BA), *Full scale tests of slots and flaps on a Heinkel He. 64 with special reference to landing.* (R. & M. No. 1713), 1936

xxxiv   The Aircraft Engineer, *Technical Literature – Summaries of A.R.C. Reports*, 29 July 1937, p. 6

xxxv   Aeronautical Research Committee, *Technical Report of the Aeronautical Research Committee for the Year 1936 Vol. I: Aerodynamics General, Performance, Airscrews, Flutter and Spinning*, 1936, p. 5

xxxvi   E.g. Taylor, H. A. *Fairey Aircraft since 1915*, Putnam, 1974, p. 234

xxxvii   Menzies, Duncan, Letter, 27 July 1976, Menzies family archive

xxxviii   James, Derek N., *Gloster Aircraft since 1917*, Putnam, 1987, p. 202

xxxix   Menzies, Duncan, *Forced landing of Vildebeest K4164, 7 January 1935* for A&AEE History, 1961, Menzies family archive

xl   Flight, *Empire Air Day: A Guide for Intending Visitors to the Various Service and Civil Aerodromes Which Will be Open to the Public Next Saturday*, 23 May 1935, p. 559

xli   Fairey, C. R., *Patent application: Blade For Airscrews And The Like*, Filed 5 June 1936, Serial No. 83,395

xlii   Götke, Lieutenant Commander Chris AFC interview with author, 20 April 2016

xliii   Brown, Captain Eric, *Wings of the Navy – Flying Allied Carrier Aircraft of WW2*, Pilot Press 1987, p. 13

xliv   *Aberdeen Press and Journal*, 'Invergordon Bride', 13 April 1936, p. 2, Menzies family archive

xlv   www.all-aero.com, *Fairey P.27/32 Battle*, www.all-aero.com/index.php/component/content/article/45-planes-d-e-f/3449-fairey-p2732-battle

xlvi   Menzies, Duncan, *Transcript, interview with Robinson, Brian, Manchester Airport archivist*, June 1988, Menzies family archive

xlvii   Webb, Raymond John, *Early Ringway*, Webstar, 1978, p. 11

xlviii   Harrison, W. A., *Database – Fairey Battle*, Aeroplane, June 2016, p. 90

xlix   Menzies, Duncan, *Transcript, interview with Robinson, Brian, Manchester Airport archivist*, June 1988, Menzies family archive

[l] Webb, Raymond John, *Early Ringway*, Webstar, 1978, p. 11

[li] Aeroplane and Armament Experimental Establishment, test report in *Fairey Fulmar, Type biographies and sources*, National Archives AVIA 46/141

[lii] *First Fulmar Squadron*, Fairey Affairs, March 1959, Menzies family archive

[liii] Captain Eric Brown, *Wings of the Navy*, Airlife Publishing 1987, p. 75

[liv] Transcript, interview with Brian Robinson, Manchester Airport archivist, June 1988, Menzies family archive

[lv] Menzies, Duncan, Letter to BBC Producer 'The Airport 50 Show', 8 June 1988, Menzies family archive

[lvi] See Royal Aircraft Establishment, *Tail buffeting on Barracuda aircraft*, (National Archives AVIA 6/10119)

[lvii] Menzies, Peter, in conversation with the author, 23 August 2011

[lviii] Menzies, Duncan, Letter, 27 July 1976, Menzies family archive

[lix] Royal Aircraft Establishment, *Tail buffeting on Barracuda aircraft*, (National Archives AVIA 6/10119)

[lx] Brown, Captain Eric, interview with the author, 26 August 2014

[lxi] E.g. Brown, Captain Eric, *Wings of the Navy*, Airlife Publishing 1987, pp. 103–6

[lxii] Brown, Captain Eric, interview with the author, 26 August 2014

[lxiii] Harrison, W. *Fairey Firefly The Operational Record*, Airlife 1992, Chapter 7 *Firefly Trainers* pp. 84–90

[lxiv] Ibid., p. 88

[lxv] Flight, *Operational Trainer*, 23 January 1947, p. 91

[lxvi] Menzies, Peter and Bennett, Mary Ann, emails to the author, 28 August 2014, 14 September 2014, 20 September 2014

[lxvii] Menzies, Peter, in conversation with the author, 20 February 2013

[lxviii] Bennett, Mary Ann, letter to the author, 16 October 2015

[lxix] Jackson, A. J., *Blackburn Aircraft Since 1909*, Putnam, 1968, p. 368

[lxx] Howard, Chris, email to the author, 19 January 2017

[lxxi] Brown, Captain Eric, interview with the author, 26 August 2014

[lxxii] *An Experimental Experience – Empire Air Day Preparations: A Visit to Martlesham and Felixstowe*, Flight, 16 May 1935, p. 532